STAND UP FOR CANADA

Leadership and the Canadian Political Crisis

kson

io   FEB 1 1993

2473

Canadian Cataloguing in Publication Data

Jackson, Robert J., 1936–
    Stand up for Canada

ISBN 0-13-841743-1

1. Canada – Politics and government – 1984–
2. Leadership. I. Jackson, Doreen, 1939–
II. Title

FC630.J32 1992   971.064'7   C92-095187-2
F1034.2.J32 1992

Prentice Hall, Inc., Englewood Cliffs, New Jersey
Prentice-Hall International, Inc., London
Prentice-Hall of Australia, Pty., Ltd., Sydney
Prentice-Hall of India Pvt., Ltd., New Delhi
Prentice-Hall of Japan, Inc., Tokyo
Prentice-Hall of Southeast Asia (Pte.) Ltd., Singapore
Editora Prentice-Hall do Brasil Ltda., Rio de Janeiro
Prentice-Hall Hispanoamericana, S.A., Mexico

ISBN: 0-13-841743-1

Design: Alex Li
Composition: Wendy Chung
Manufacturing Buyer: Anita Boyle

1 2 3 4 5   IG   96 95 94 93 92

Printed and bound in Canada by Imprimerie Gagné Ltée

CONTENTS

PREFACE

Canada is approaching a watershed in its history. Constitutional confusion and chicanery have produced political necrobiosis. Our so-called political leaders are stripping the federal government of its ability to make decisions for the country, playing to social divisions, and fragmenting the party system. For all Canadians who place a strong, united country above parochial rivalries, it is imperative to participate in the next general election and demand more from our political leaders. We need leaders who will stand up for Canada and guide it through the difficult years ahead, years which are bound to be difficult because of the corrosive conditions created by the current government.

When we first thought about writing this book we had in mind a mixture of history, description and analysis about Canada's eighteen Prime Ministers, but the maddening behaviour of present-day politicians forced us to reconsider our task. This is not a book of documented scholarship; instead, it is a volume from two Canadians who care deeply about their country and believe that the role of citizens is to be involved in the process.

Given the present Canadian situation it would be improper, even distasteful, to stand back, fearful and on guard against any criticism of our point of view. The thought that the country could survive the constitutional reform process only to break up after it is finished calls on everyone to judge those responsible and demand more of leadership. In the coming crisis there will be a high cost to the country if those who have been blessed by the advantages of life in Canada remain silent and paralyzed on the sidelines.

Today's crop of leaders and lesser politicians make the old joke about the doctor, architect and politician worth repeating. Debating which of them represented the earliest profession, the doctor said that the Bible proved medicine was the oldest profession because the first thing God did was perform an operation on Adam to create Eve. Not to be outdone by this rib-tickler the architect replied that no, the first thing in the Bible is that God created the beautiful heavens and earth from darkness and chaos. This triumph showed that architecture was the oldest profession. The politican won the debate, however, by asking his two colleagues just who they thought created chaos in the first place!

Possibly we expect too much of our politicans. They do not need to be saints. But are Canadian politicians standing up for Canada rather than their own ethnic, provincial, regional or special interests? We think few are. Instead of building on what we have already, many of them wish to dismantle the institutions which have given us one of the most properous, free and just countries in the world. They are constitutional pyromaniacs.

There are grave flaws in our constitution and institutions but our so-called leaders are producing the conditions for a breaking up of the country just to get an agreement in time to save their own electoral skins. Amending a constitution is not, and should not be, easy. It has to be like the slow, patient and frustrating sawing of thick boards. It is sweaty work and not to many people's taste.

Leadership is the issue in Canada and it can be addressed immediately. Unlike constitution-building which — as all Canadians know by now — is by nature laborious and boring, an election can be exhilarating. Join with us in categorizing Canada's current leaders into friends and enemies of the country. When the general election is called, let us dissect the leadership qualities of the contenders and choose the best from among Canada's friends. We need to quell the simmering cauldron of discontent that exists today. Let those who stand for the politics of difference and division confront those who stand up for Canada.

In writing this book we had the help of many friends and experts. Michael Kaduck stood by the project from beginning to end, contributing wisely to the development, research and writing of several sections of the book. Marion Armstrong and Ruth Bradley-St-Cyr aided greatly in the final writing by their careful attention to detail and composition. Tanya Long's enthusiasm for the project, and excellent editorial assistance, allowed us to meet a tight production schedule. We thank all four for sitting down to work quickly and diligently on *Stand Up For Canada*. Neither they nor other friends who read the manuscript are responsible for the final judgments of the text. We take that duty on our shoulders with no regret.

This book is dedicated to the next generation of leaders who must hope that there will, indeed, still be a Canada for which they *can* stand up.

Robert J. Jackson
Doreen Jackson
Mistra, Quebec.
August, 1992

1 The Coming Crisis: Leadership In A Divided Society

"Awake, my country, the hour is great with change!
 Under this gloom which yet obscures the land,
From ice-blue strait and stern Laurentian range
 To where giant peaks our western bounds command,
A deep voice stirs, vibrating in men's ears..."

> — *Sir Charles G.D. Roberts*
> *"An Ode for the Canadian Confederacy"*
> *(1886)*

Canadian politicians are provoking a crisis in Canada. Having brought the country to the verge of disintegration over constitutional reform, they are pandering to sectional interests in order to maintain their positions in office and their power bases in Ottawa and the provincial capitals. Led by Prime Minister Brian Mulroney, they act as if the country were theirs to experiment with.

There are three conditions propelling the country relentlessly toward weak, stalemate government: Canadians have accepted an unworthy vision of the country based on ethnicity, provincialism and special interests, thereby deepening regional divisions; Canadian political institutions have become flawed over time because of Prime Ministerial dominance and the inability to amend the Constitution to reflect current political concerns; and, finally, the country is handicapped with weak leadership.

1

These three conditions have combined to create symptoms of the crisis to come. They are familiar to all observant Canadians. One symptom is the interminable, indecisive debates about constitutional reform, in which no leaders stand up for Canada as a whole; another is low public confidence and anger about institutions and leaders.

Canada is passing through this symptom stage to a more dangerous condition of which our leaders seem blissfully ignorant. While pressures for immediate resolution of the constitutional debates are distracting attention from the bigger picture, Canada is about to be saddled with a decentralized Constitution. And, at the same time, fragmented, regional voting behaviour is about to revolutionize the country's political party system from two-and-a-half nationally-based parties to one with five regionally-based parties. A general election must be held by November 1993. It could leave the country with a combination of fragmented parties and a weakened, decentralized system that will bring effective government to a halt.

Constitutional decentralization and a fragmented party system will create a splintered Parliament with weak, minority governments. A crisis will be upon us. The federal government will no longer be able to provide the kind of positive guidance and progressive atmosphere which is necessary to militate against weaknesses in the economy or to continue building Canada's social security net for the disadvantaged of our society. Canada as we know it will have been destroyed. Provinces or regions will easily find reasons to go their own separate ways.

A DANGEROUS IDEOLOGY

Current political behaviour is buttressed by a new and corrosive ideology, subtly encouraged by Prime Minister Brian Mulroney and his Conservative government. It is an ideology of "difference" which is not unique to Canada.

Internationally, the Cold War has ended with the termination of left-right ideological divisions. Fascism and communism, the challengers of democracy, have been discredited. But peace and harmony still elude the globe. Today's world abounds with divisions due to ethnic hatred, regional antagonism and sometimes-violent nationalism.

Political leaders around the world are propagating a new ideology of "difference" to manipulate the emotions and actions of the masses, and Canada is following that trend. Canadians of different origins, cultures, languages and regions are dividing over the very nature and definition of the country. The Canadian multi-ethnic state and its political framework of federalism is undergoing the supreme test: to hold together as one country despite deep internal contradictions, confusion and even hatred.

A new group-centred ideological orthodoxy has developed in Canada; since groups are all-important, nothing critical can be said about them or their goals. This thinking dominates and permeates all aspects of Canadian society. Standing up for individuals and all of Canada is somehow without coinage or worth. The politically correct view which now predominates is that *diversity* is the holy of holies in the Temple of Canadian Nationalism; it is tantamount to treason to see Canada as more than an irascible collection of groups, provinces, regions, ethnic affiliations and special interests. Diversity, however, is but one of the building blocks of the country, an important source of Canadian identity, pride and unity, but only one small part of the structure itself.

World history shows that some states remain united even though they embrace vast differences. The United States is one such example. Its citizens conceive of themselves as part of the same "nation" or "melting pot." Americans have built their country through shared experiences and commitment to similar political ideals and values.

Canada is less of a melting pot and more of a "Christmas cake" than its illustrious southern neighbour. The Canadian approach has been to encourage different cultures to co-exist side by side in harmony and tolerance. In Canada, however, the pressure for provincial and ethnic distinctiveness and special interests is beginning to undermine the belief in the state as a whole. Most ordinary Canadians are preoccupied with improving their own personal lives. But under the spell of their often self-appointed leaders they are manipulated into depression and insecurity based on declining confidence in the importance of the individual and the country as a whole. These so-called leaders have no compunctions about playing to ethnic or regional interests at the expense of the welfare of individuals and even the country.

The belief that Canada is nothing but different groups and regions joined in "a community of communities," to use Joe Clark's expression, is destructive. It perpetuates antagonism, magnifies differences, segregates people, and leads to arguments for aboriginal and regional alienation and Quebec separatism. It is a recipe for tribalism that is readily used by special interest group leaders to further their own causes at the expense of the whole.

Current leaders, by accepting a philosophy of difference, have placed Canadians who take issue with the Conservative government's decentralizing proposals on the defensive. Those who disagree are branded as "against Quebec" or "against the West" or "against the native peoples," even though their objections are based on the fact that they are "for" Canada.

The fact is, the current Constitution has served Canada well. Under it, Canada grew from a tiny, insignificant and backward colony to a vast country spanning the width of an entire continent — a country which today is a member of the Group of Seven largest industrialized states in the world, and is recognized around the globe as "world class."

Yet in spite of these accomplishments Canadians are continually being told by self-serving politicans that "Canada does not work." Their discordant tune is chanted well beyond our borders. The country is "not working" so we must "overhaul the constitution," "decentralize," "separate," "declare independence unilaterally," or "radically reconstitute federalism." The list of cures seems endless, and they all call for changes that will radically alter the Canada we know and love and which currently stands at the top of the UN's Human Development Index. A study for the Business Council on National Issues said Canada needs "radical surgery" and might "die" on the operating table. If they have their way, our leaders will reduce Canada and Canadians to a petty, bickering gaggle of parochial units incapable of surviving on their own. In short, the cure may be worse than the disease.

It has also become routine for community leaders to advocate violence to get their own way — to "hold a knife at the throat" of other Canadians, or hold a gun to Canada's head. And it is considered normal to manipulate statistical data and figures to prove opposing points of view, with no regard for an accurate over-all assessment. One week a research group claimed that federalism had been financially profitable for Quebec. The next week another group gave figures to show that it had not. The first group based its case on a ten-year period, the latter on the last two years.

Some otherwise quite rational Canadians are so convinced by this rhetoric that they argue over how the national debt will be divided up after Quebec separates, or whether there will need to be a corridor through Quebec so that the Maritime provinces can still be linked to the remainder of the country. That such topics should be taken seriously in a country of Canada's stature is absurd. Our energies should be used to solve *real* problems.

CANADA DOES WORK!

Canadians are periodically surprised to hear objective and respected foreign institutions singing Canada's praises. The 1990 data from the Organization for Economic Cooperation and Development placed

Canada 4th in per capita Gross Domestic Product (see Table 1). UN statistics based on 1990 data declare that Canada has the second highest standard of living in the world (see Table 2) and the highest Human Development Standard (see Table 3). This placement is based on data which combines average income with such factors as health, education, a good physical environment, and freedom of action and expression. And equally important, comparative studies of political freedoms around the world continually applaud Canada as one of the freest countries on earth.

Table 1:1   Per Capita Gross Domestic Product for World's Top Ten Countries*

1.	United States	21,449
2.	Switerzerland	20,997
3.	Luxembourg	19,340
4.	Canada	19,120
5.	Germany	18,291
6.	Japan	17,634
7.	France	17,431
8.	Sweden	16,867
9.	Denmark	16,765
10.	Finland	16,435

*GDP 1990, using purchasing power parity exchange rates.
   Source: Organization for Economic Cooperation and Development, 1990.

Table 1:2   Standard of Living for World's Top 10 States*

1.	Japan	0.993
2.	Canada	0.983
3.	Iceland	0.983
4.	Sweden	0.982
5.	Switzerland	0.981
6.	Norway	0.978
7.	United States	0.976
8.	Netherlands	0.976
9.	Australia	0.973
10.	France	0.971

*U.N. Human Development Index adjusted for life expectancy and literacy.
  Source: United Nations, 1990.

Table 1:3   Human Development Index

Country		Human Development Index*
1.	Canada	0.982
2.	Japan	0.981
3.	Norway	0.978
4.	Switzerland	0.977
5.	Sweden	0.976
6.	USA	0.976
7.	Australia	0.971
8.	France	0.969
9.	Netherlands	0.968
10.	United Kingdom	0.962

*The Human Development Index includes the following: life expectancy at birth, 1990;
  adult literacy rate, 1990; mean years index; educational attainment; real GDP per capita 1989; and adjusted real GDP.
Source: United Nations, *Human Development Report 1992* (New York: Oxford University Press, 1992), p. 127

Canada works so well that it is world class. That is clear to everyone but those tepid and tentative Canadians who are preoccupied with pursuing ethnic, regional or special interests or searching every nook and cranny for their own personal identities. Collectively, Canadians have a remarkable lack of faith in themselves and their country. Abroad, in international institutions, we calmly and wisely help to find and implement positive solutions to other people's problems. We need look no further than our much-sought-after peace-keeping forces for proof of our abilities. At home, however, wisdom and ability fail us, calm and a positive approach evaporate and our own problems seem insurmountable. The Canadian national identity will be a problem until enough *individual* Canadians acquire self-confident identities of their own. That is difficult to achieve in a self-deprecating milieu where creativity and talent tend to be recognized abroad long before they are grudgingly admitted at home.

It should be a primary function of leadership to stimulate a collective awareness of the great value of this country. Unfortunately, however, in times of difficulties — particularly those which are government-generated — opportunism tends to take over and public figures prevaricate and exaggerate complaints to create the impression that they put a very low value on Canada as we know it.

The scenario of partisan parochialism is all too familiar. Take a random few days in 1992, for example: Benoît Bouchard, the senior Quebec cabinet minister in Ottawa, proffered that he did not know how he would vote if Quebec held a referendum on sovereignty, implying that Canada is not worth saving in its present form; Alberta Premier Don Getty said he was willing to risk a referendum on independence in Quebec if he did not get a Triple-E senate; and Premier Bob Rae of Ontario opined that Ontario "feels the bonds of nationhood differently" since Ottawa reduced the growth rate of federal financial transfers to the province.

Then, according to established tradition, when public opinion was sufficiently fractured and disillusioned that the very unity of the country was in question, the federal government threw millions of dollars into a massive ad campaign featuring smiling, multi-ethnic faces and Canada geese to convince us how lucky we are to be

Canadians. The government was once more stimulating a kind of pouty pride that it could turn on or off to suit its own electoral interests.

The naysayers' charge that Canada "does not work" is, demonstrably, rhetorical nonsense. The world abounds in poor, unstable countries plagued with war, famine and poverty, governed by dictators, military governments, theocracies and other forms of authoritarian rule. Even among the democratically stable systems, few, if any, have the prosperity, respect or influence Canada enjoys.

Canadians should not allow falsehoods and half truths to spread unchallenged. Canada does work and it works well. Parliament works smoothly and democratically. Canadians are among the most prosperous, freest, best educated and healthiest people in the world. The French culture and language in Canada is not just alive but thriving in a huge continent surrounded by English.

Separatists, regionalists and doomsters should be challenged to find a country anywhere that works any better. Before any constitutional experiments are put into practice Canadians should use objective criteria to compare Canada with other states. They should, for once, cease and desist from parochial introspection, look beyond their country's borders and see Canada in a comparative perspective. Acknowledging Canada's benefits may prevent us from mistakenly embarking on downward mobility for the whole country.

Canada is clearly not paradise. Governments must be constantly adapting to new social conditions. The world is changing, and Canada is too. Many reforms must be reflected in laws and institutions. To paraphrase a famous Italian author, for things to remain the same here some changes will have to be made. But they need not be rushed, or implemented by way of a mammoth, ambiguous "package" deal. The Constitution we have does not need to be torched by over-zealous constitutional pyromaniacs. Some amendments are needed, but the *urgency* and *extent* of these changes have been fabricated.

THE GREAT CANADIAN MYTH

Today, in spite of our relatively advantaged position in the world, it is now a commonly accepted myth that Canadians never developed an all-embracing national consciousness because of differences of ethnicity, language and region. Proponents of this myth say that Canadians have little in common, but live on interlinked islands of special interests, and therefore do not enjoy a common purpose and shared experience which can counterbalance the strains inflamed by the ideology of "difference." Followed to its logical conclusion, this view suggests that eventually the country could fragment into competing micro-states.

This is an unduly pessimistic and myopic view. Canadians should wake up and recognize that we do have a shared history and heritage. Despite the mixed French, English, aboriginal and multi-ethnic character of the country, our citizens have fought and died together in two world wars, carved new territories out of the West and North, and developed unique cultural, economic, and social policies which have held the country together and made it prosper. On the international stage Canadians have helped to form the United Nations, have lent a hand to needy people around the world, and have provided an opportunity to refugees to live in the shelter of a peaceful and bountiful country. Suffering and striving together in a harsh northern climate and sharing common hopes and fears have made us a much more united people than cynics acknowledge.

Canadians also share common values and ideals, such as individual rights and freedoms, equality of opportunity, fairness, protected minimum standards of health facilities and old-age security. The culture is characterized by a set of assumptions about the role of the state in Canada. All of our Prime Ministers, with the apparent exception of Brian Mulroney, have accepted the public's belief in the need for a strong central government, reasonable state intervention in the economy, and the requirement of an expanding social security net to support the poorer, weaker and older among us.

The culture is a tolerant one but this does not mean that there are no problems; there are. However, Canadians of different ethnic, cultural and language backgrounds are bound together in a tapestry of tolerance, with their differences blending into one colourful whole — Canada.

ETHNICITY, PROVINCIALISM AND NATIONALISM

Canada is undergoing a metamorphosis the outcome of which is uncertain. A beautiful, new state may be born, new countries may emerge, or a hideous, racist creature may creep from the constitutional and political morass.

The transformation of the country is taking place because of a contest between those who favour a strong, united Canada and those who prefer a loosely-bound country constructed from its many parts and special interests. A rabid cult of provincialism, ethnicity and interest group self-assertion is flourishing, much of which was nourished by the shameful treatment of minorities in the past.

Provincial interests, ethnic differences and pressure groups have not always been handled appropriately. Canada has many skeletons in its historical closet which foster regional and ethnic resentment. From the maltreatment of aboriginal peoples to the hanging of Louis Riel, to the negative reception of French-speaking Canadians in English-speaking parts of the country to the imposition of the *War Measures Act*, Canada has committed crimes against its citizens which should not be forgotten. As well, intolerance and violence towards visible and not-so-visible minorities have run the gamut from the "No Irish or Dogs" signs of the early 1800s to the internment of Japanese-Canadians and the denial of refuge to the Jews of Europe during World War II to the "Paki-busting" of the 1970s. Such racism has surfaced often in Canadian society, always focussing on the most recent immigrants and always intensifying during times of economic stress.

Canadians need to establish a balanced view of the good and bad in their country's history, and not be led down stony paths by those who would sow seeds of hatred among disparate groups in order to highlight the triumphs of their own clan or disguise the weaknesses in their arguments. There is a profound need to celebrate the greatness of Canada and to fight against its decomposition. Democracy, freedom, tolerance and human rights are ideals which sometimes slip from our grasp but we must make every effort to hang on to them.

There is as well a need to re-consider the Canadian concept of unity in diversity. A rapid influx of immigrants has affected the definition of what it means to be Canadian. The changing population composition has created a more heterogeneous and vibrant society, but it has also enhanced the difficulty of maintaining a viable country. So-called new Canadians come from so many varied cultural and linguistic backgrounds that they sometimes lack the historical consciousness of how Canada has functioned in the past.

In welcoming and accommodating these new Canadians, we must keep Canada as a whole in focus. An ethnic-centred view of Canada leads to the belief that Canada is nothing but the sum of its parts — that roots of ethnicity, race, language and colour are the bases of Canada. This pathogenic view has recently become the sum total of Canadian thought and reasoning about politics. It is based on a philosophy which, if left to grow, will, like a cancer, lead to the destruction of Canadian consciousness.

Many factors have given rise to this philosophy that Canada is nothing but a chain of interlinked provinces, ethnic groups and special interests. Some of them are old, some new. Provincial politicans have *always* built their careers around arguing how unique their provinces are. Ethnic leaders have built their reputations on encouraging distinctiveness in their own groups and, sometimes, mistrust of others. And interest-group leaders make it their business to promote their own cause above all others in the belief that the squeaking wheel gets the grease. Today, hard economic times encourage people to retrench and think small; how do *I* survive the recession is a more important question than how does *Canada* survive.

During the past few years political dialogue in Canada has developed an inward, morose character. Quebec separation is discussed in terms of probability rather than possibility; parochial regionalism is rampant; interest groups are circling like vultures to pick what they can from the not yet dead carcass of the country. Academics and others write about how Canada is going to "collapse" or "self-destruct." Some cynics even argue egregiously that Canada would be better off if Quebec did separate.

Whenever separatism is flourishing in Quebec one particular weakness hampers finding a solution. Discussion is always put in terms of French and English Canada: "English Canada" rejects this or that proposal from Quebec. This is nonsense. While Quebec makes demands for the majority of "French Canada," there is no possible mechanism for "English Canada" to accept or reject anything. The federal system of government is not set up that way. First of all, everyone outside of Quebec is not "English," and secondly, they cannot speak with one voice because there is no single, official spokesperson.

Under no circumstances can the federal government be the voice of "English Canada." The federal government represents *all* of Canada, including Quebec. The current Prime Minister and his Cabinet are buttressed by MPs, the majority of whom are elected from the province of Quebec. It is incumbent on Prime Minister Mulroney and Leader of the Opposition Jean Chrétien — who are both from Quebec — to make this clear. They represent Quebec just as much as they do the rest of the country.

Canadian leaders today, who should be the first to speak for Canada, concentrate too much on provincial, ethnic and interest-group distinctiveness rather than a common philosophy of the country as a whole. Indeed some unscrupulous politicians have taken to sanctioning and deepening divisions in society for their own ends,

13

driving wedges into the fissures of Canada's already divided society. When they build their careers on we-they, French-English, native-non-native, West-East dichotomies they increase the tendency to view Canada in terms of its differences rather than its similarities. They are encouraging groups to see themselves in terms of their victimization and to pursue their own particular interests rather than the common interest of society as a whole.

Canada has survived and even flourished for 125 years. Yet, at the very time when it should be celebrating that anniversary, it is facing divisions which threaten its very existence. A sign along highway 7 in Ontario reads "125 years and still no responsible government." The sentiment is widely felt. What is new at this point in our history is vision-less leadership. Political leaders no longer explain what it is to be a Canadian over and above provincial and ethnic differences and special interests. Few herald the equality of all human beings in the country whatever their language, culture, race or gender. Few extol the dignity and worth of each and every individual. Few explain to the people what is required of them to keep together a thriving, highly differentiated society.

The field has been left wide open to the leaders of ethnic, provincial and special interest groups who are taking advantage of the declining confidence in our future as one country. In short, no one stands up for Canada.

LET'S BE MORE PRECISE

One elementary step that can be taken to eliminate friction between different language groups, particularly French, English and native peoples, is to ensure that Canadians all mean the same thing when they use words. When words like "nation" in English and "*nation*" in French are used there is a tendency to think they mean the same thing because they are spelled the same way. They do not. Crucial words like "nation" and "state" also mean different things to different people even when they speak the same language. As Mark Twain once noted, the difference between the right word and almost the right word is as great as the difference between lightning and the lightning bug. Canadians are politically illiterate in this sense, and constantly misunderstand and insult each other when there is no need to.

Canada is one state with one legal and jurisdictional structure. Within it there can be any number of nations. State boundaries provide a framework within which to balance the competing claims and interests of the individuals, groups and nations within it.

A nation in its sociological sense means an emotional or spiritual attachment; its presence is usually determined by the degree of "we-ness" in a group or community. In Canada, the aboriginal peoples constitute a nation. So do French Canadians. While it is not possible to permit sovereign states to exist within the Canadian state, it is reasonable to grant greater degrees of freedom to nations within our borders.

But recognition of group rights should never be allowed to *replace* the idea of a *Canadian* nation which includes us all, regardless of ethnic heritage, native language, skin colour, religion or residence. The over-arching political culture which binds us together emotionally and spiritually must be protected and nourished.

What this points to is a need to define words and be precise about them in order to avoid misunderstandings. At the very practical level, clear definitions of phrases such as "distinct society" and "self-government" are essential before they are embedded in the Constitution if we are to avoid an escalation of expectations that cannot, or will not, be achieved.

WHY DON'T CANADIANS STAND UP FOR ONE CANADA?

There are many factors to blame for Canadians' contemporary and widespread lack of appreciation of their common heritage and communal interests. Gravely flawed institutions is one of them. Inadequate leadership is another.

Canada inherited deep and persistent cleavages based on ethnic, linguistic and regional fault lines. To deal with them, Canadians established a hybrid parliamentary and federal system of government. That system is not well suited to a period of overlapping problems and weak political leadership. Its parliamentary-cabinet form of government combined with a highly decentralized federal system makes it difficult for political leaders to deal with many complex issues at the same time. The problems are compounded when the country lacks a government with strong leadership. A country like Canada needs particularly competent leaders at the centre of government. It is important to establish institutions which will make periods of low leadership competence less dangerous for the country.

Today governmental institutions are experiencing difficulty balancing the demands of parochial interests with the needs of Canadian society as a whole. Major flaws have developed in the country's political institutions.

The governmental system has changed over time to weaken Parliament to the benefit of the Prime Minister and his coterie of assistants. This has deprived Canadians of the feeling that their government is fair, responsive and democratic. And it has left the system vulnerable to irresponsible leaders. The executive branch now dominates Parliament to the point that the country can barely withstand a period of weak leadership. In response to this, pressures are building to weaken the federal system by decentralizing and transferring many of its powers to the provinces.

Parties no longer aggregate interests and represent Canadians across the whole country. They do not ensure the strong, unifying force at the centre that a sprawling, diverse state needs to hold it together against a tide of competing interests.

The test of political leadership is how to manage the country in order to reduce or smooth over, and certainly not widen or deepen, societal cleavages. As the following chapters demonstrate, seventeen Prime Ministers have shown this quality — one has not. Current political leaders are not strong enough to withstand the assaults by political interests from within and economic pressures from without. Canada has never experienced such a drought of leadership at such a crucial time. We have political pygmies leading the country when we need giants.

Leaders can be regarded as friends or enemies of Canada. Friends stand up for national unity and a strong central government, while enemies seek to divide and separate.

On these two criteria Brian Mulroney is already recognized as a weak Prime Minister. During his tenure Canadian government has been damaged almost beyond repair. Unless he salvages the Constitution and miraculously avoids creating conditions for the break-up of Canada, he will go down in history as the country's worst-ever Prime Minister. The mish-mash of decentralizing changes presented in the August 1992 constitutional proposal currently place him squarely in the enemy camp.

Looking across the panorama of other would-be leaders today we see that they, too, may be characterzed as friends or enemies. Jean Chrétien and Audry McLaughlin are both friends of Canada, though they have some serious weaknesses. In the past, they have both defended strong federalism. However, by supporting Mulroney's constitutional deal they have abandoned their principles and are inadvertently aiding Canada's enemies.

Preston Manning, Lucien Bouchard and Jacques Parizeau are outright enemies. They rejected the August 1992 constitutional arrangements, but for their own political ends. Premier Robert Bourassa has long been a fence-sitting enigma. In his support for the constitutional deal he may yet undo his own political career and damage Canada's viability.

The fact that politicians and those who live off them — communicators, journalists and the like — seem unaware of the *interac-*

tion between parochial interests and weak leadership forced us to consider the crisis that is being invited to Canada. The Quebec challenge of independence has bewildered Canadian politicians — they stumble from event to event and policy to policy. The country is waltzing its way into disunity and even partition, while the politicians focus on their own roles in the political system. Everyone wants to lead but no one seems to know the steps.

During the next year Canadians will have at least three opportunities to judge their leaders. On October 26, 1992 they will be able to make their views known about the constitutional referendum. In voting they should consider leadership as well as judge the details of the Charlottetown accord. If the referendum passes, they will get a second opportunity to exert their will during the discussions of the eleven legislatures on the precise amendments to the Constitution. By November 1993 there must be a general election in Canada, at which time Canadians will be able to throw out the present rascals or reward them for their political helmsmanship.

It is time for all Canadians to expose the enemies of Canada for what they are and to demand that they put Canada first. This is dramatic. Canada is approaching a crisis in its history — the constitutional dance of death has begun. It is not yet too late, but it is the eleventh hour... 11:30 in Newfoundland.

2 Canada's Widening Fault Lines

*"Canada is a dream in the making...we have a lot to share.
Sharing: that's what a confederation is about."*

— **Roch Carrier, Canadian Living,**
(September 1992)

All states have societal fault lines, or points of division, that lie
dormant only to erupt during times of stress and change. In Canada,
the major fault lines are deep and persistent. Most have been present
since Confederation in 1867 or before. But never since 1867 have they
threatened the country more than during Brian Mulroney's Conservative government when the flawed process of constitution-making
divided Canadians into squabbling factions.

The most serious and persistent internal faults are along ethnic
and regional lines, the most prominent of which separate French and
English, native peoples and other Canadians, Westerners, central
Canadians and Maritimers, dividing the country and setting Canadian
against Canadian. French separatists in Quebec feel swamped lin-
guistically as a tiny pond of francophones in a North American sea
of anglophones and are demanding their own country. Westerners are
alienated. They feel outnumbered demographically, economically,

and politically by the electoral power of central Canadians and want increased regional powers to compensate. Native peoples want undefined, open-ended self-government as a political step, as they see it, to return to the pride and self-determination of the days before European settlement.

In the past, leadership was often barely adequate to manage such divisions. Today, it is clearly inadequate, and Canada is paying the price. The vision which guides today's political leaders defines the country in terms of its various parts rather than as a whole. Canadians are encouraged to see themselves first and foremost as members of some group in the Canadian mosaic. It is an attractive concept in the abstract, but in practice it is extremely divisive. "Leadership" is always available to rouse the masses and herd them into hostile groups which respond to appeals to historical injustices, some current unfairness, or ethnic differences. Each group fights for a better foothold at the expense of the others, and no one stands up for Canada as a whole.

All three major fault lines are involved in the constitutional crisis which began when Prime Minister Brian Mulroney set out to offer a new deal to Quebec. New arrangements had to be formulated to placate Quebec after Prime Minister Trudeau patriated the Constitution in 1982 without that province's consent. The negotiations presented the perfect opportunity for Quebec to make unilateral demands, and also for the other provinces, regions and native peoples to bargain hard for themselves. The leaders of the various groups have launched out on a bonanza of self-indulgence, dragging out negotiations until Canadians can hardly bear to listen any more, all the while playing brinksmanship with the very existence of the country.

Selfish parochialism has created a whirlpool of discontent, drawing the country closer to the vortex of destruction. Political leaders, with a shallow collective sense of self, and a strong desire for self-preservation, dither, looking for oars and life preservers. But Canada need not be drawn into the abyss. The first step is to recognize the fragility of the fault lines; the second is to broaden our horizons and reject the ideology of difference; the third is to demand that leaders refrain from exploiting differences, and instead create policies that strengthen the national culture that already exists. Collectively, we are responsible for having created a hollow centre instead of a wellspring of creative leadership to direct this country.

ETHNIC FAULT LINES

Canadians are not, and never have been, a homogeneous whole. And they are becoming ever more diverse as a people. Earlier generations put Canada first and built a great country based on tolerance and generosity. Current ethnic and regional divisions are often distorted by myths and selective memories. Today, many Canadians have changed the way they think about their differences, seeing themselves first and foremost in terms of smaller group identities.

Two Solitudes: The French-English Partnership

The French-English relationship in Canada extends back to the earliest colonial days. After a century and a half of independent existence in America, the French were conquered by the English in 1760. As a conquered people, with the humiliation which that implies, they did not integrate with the victors but formed an isolated and rural society, living in small parish units whose economic activity centered on the family farm. An initial strategy of *la survivance*, resisting assimilation by the English, was directed by the Roman Catholic Church.

French immigration virtually ceased after the Conquest, while over the next decades immigrants poured in from Britain and the United States. By the time of Confederation in 1867 there were nearly twice as many English as French in the new country.

Industrialization and the so-called "Quiet Revolution" dramatically changed the environment in Quebec. By the second half of the 20th century, values in the province began to shift radically from rural to urban, and from religious to secular. By 1971 Quebec's population was over 80% urban, technological changes had altered the educational and social structure, and a new administrative elite had grown up to manage the new state powers which emerged with control over education, welfare and medical care — previously church-run institutions.

The impact of these changes on French Canadians was profound. They were forced to emerge from isolation and increase their direct contact with other groups, particularly English- Canadians and Americans who owned most of the new urban, industrial society. What they realized when they emerged from their agrarian cocoon was that Quebec's economy was characterized by a predominance of non-French capital and non-French ownership in large corporations. The export-oriented, resource-based corporations tended to be under American or multi-national control. Modern light industry (such as electronics) was largely owned by anglo-Canadians. French Canadians predominated in labour intensive, lower productivity industries such as textiles, leather processing and food processing. Financial institutions (stock market, bonds and securities, banks, trusts, life insurance) were predominantly anglo-Canadian controlled.

Impotent and frustrated by their inability to rapidly join the economic and political elite of their province, the hostility of many Quebeckers grew. In the 1960s, the "Quiet Revolution" eventually blossomed into an outright challenge to Canadian federalism and the very unity of the Canadian state. Socio-economic changes did not ameliorate Quebec's financial problems; throughout the 1970s about a third of all unemployed Canadians continued to be found in that province.

In the 1980s Quebec made incredible strides, and by 1992 the tables have turned. Quebec has a thriving, internationally recognized

French culture — the Montreal Symphony Orchestra, for example, is reputed to be the best "French" orchestra in the world. The French language has never been more significant in the daily life of Quebeckers. The province also has a powerful business sector; Quebec-based corporations have international stature — powerful enough that some business leaders encourage Quebec to leave Canada and strike out on its own.

Myths and Sins of the Past

The Fathers of Confederation created what D'Arcy McGee called a "political nation," giving Canada every power a political nation needed to thrive. George Etienne Cartier negotiated for Quebec and gave his strong support to this vision. He saw it as the responsibility of the provinces to preserve what he called "cultural nations" — cultures imported from England, Ireland, Scotland and pre-revolutionary France.

After Cartier's death, however, his Quebec critics claimed that Confederation was really a "compact" between French and English nations. This myth flourished, nourishing the notion of "two founding nations" which provided French Canadians with a collective claim to equality rather than simple minority status within Canada. The word "compact" also implied a right to secede from the bargain.

Discord between the English and French has not been constant since 1867; nor is it just a recent phenomenon. The rights of French-speaking Canadians have often been infringed, but episodes of unrest have been interspersed with relatively prolonged periods of good relations. It is generally accepted today that the Confederation arrangement was a bargain between French and English to create one strong political unit, a country which would protect the rights and assist the advancement of two culturally diverse peoples. English- and French-language communities were to be protected. But it did not work that way in practice. From the outset, English was a legal language in the Quebec legislature and courts. In the other provinces, however, the practice until the 1940s was for English-speaking Canadians, wherever they were in the majority, to deprive French-speaking Canadian minorities of public school facilities in their native language, and to refuse them the use of their language in government institutions.

Several historical crises marked the breakdown of good will between English and French in Canada and stimulated the growth of frustration and eventually separatist movements. Although they are given relatively cursory recognition by Canadians outside Quebec, French Canadians dwell upon these events and find in them the emotional justification for the need to defend themselves as a distinct, cultural minority in Canada.

For example, the Manitoba Schools Question represented a bitter and significant loss of French and Catholic rights outside Quebec. Because of its large French-speaking community, Manitoba was created in 1870 on the same basis as Quebec, with Roman Catholic schools and bilingual education. However, by 1885, French-speaking Métis (part French and part aboriginal) in the West were being swamped by English-speaking settlers. Métis leader Louis Riel led a rebellion against the government to protest the loss of land to the new immigrants. Eastern Canada sent troops to quell the disturbance, and Riel was defeated and executed. French Canadians grieved for Riel as a patriot who died in the struggle to preserve the "Frenchness" of his people. English Canadians, until very recently, dismissed him as a traitor or a madman. French and English ethnic groups were polarized, and the stage was set for the limitation of French language rights in Manitoba.

Five years after the Riel rebellion, the government of Manitoba established a completely non-sectarian educational system in which Roman Catholic schools no longer received provincial aid. Despite intervention by the British courts the affront to French-speaking Manitobans was upheld. The Liberals, supported by Quebec, won the

1896 election and then turned around and prevented legislation which would have protected French-Canadian interests in Manitoba.

Manitoba was not the only province to break the Confederation bargain in the field of education. Practically every other province also infringed French rights. Even in the federal government, where the *British North America Act* had stated the right of both groups to function in debates, records, journals and courts in their own language, government employees were able to function largely in English only.

These were serious infractions of the spirit of the Constitution concerning French minority rights. The loss of French rights outside Quebec encouraged the virtual abandonment by the Québécois of French Canadians outside their province, and the gradual assertion of Quebec nationalism rather than French-Canadian nationalism.

Two other historical events provided emotional fuel for nationalist fires in Quebec. Both centred on the conscription crises which erupted during the two World Wars.

The 1917 federal election on the conscription issue divided the country along linguistic lines; every riding in which French was the majority language voted against the government and conscription. Pro-conscription forces won. The war ended before conscription could be enacted, but it left a legacy of bitterness in Quebec. In the next federal election the pro-conscription Conservatives were trounced in the province and the Liberals formed a minority government.

Yet the conscription crisis was replayed during World War II. This time, in 1942, the Liberal government of Mackenzie King held a plebiscite, or non-binding referendum, on the matter. Following a bitter campaign 85% of French-speaking Quebec voted against conscription, while English-speaking Canada voted overwhelmingly in favour. The war ended before the conscripts were sent into battle, but the apparent impotence of the French in face of the English majority decision remained as a humiliating residue and fueled Quebec nationalism.

The contemporary issues of Quebec separatism must be seen on this broad historical and pan-Canadian canvas as well as in the context of changing attitudes inside the province. These past grievances justify concern for the preservation of the French language and culture which has often been manifested in Quebec nationalism. French-speaking Quebeckers continue to need reassurance and protection against possible infringements on their community because of their minority status in Canada.

Nationalism in Quebec

Nationalism has appeared in many forms since the modern state emerged in the 16th and 17th centuries in Europe. It has been used as a justification for economic expansionism and imperialism, and as an ideology to espouse the superiority of a particular people over another, as in Nazi Germany. In most cases, nationalism was used to integrate members of a future state. In other cases, however, territorially concentrated ethnic minorities already inside a state have sought increased self-determination and even total independence. Quebec has shown both these latter tendencies.

After Canadian Confederation, two strains of nationalism developed in Quebec, one inward looking, one outward. The former called for a rural vision of Catholic, anti-materialist values, and on occasion resulted in proposals for an inward-looking, corporatist and authoritarian solution to the Quebec situation. The latter strain called for a pan-Canadian vision and an equal partnership between English and French Canada.

The inward-looking strain was found in the Union Nationale governments of Maurice Duplessis and his followers, 1936-39 and 1944-60. The outward-looking strain was typified by the Quebec Liberal Party which Jean Lesage led to victory in 1960, and which guided the "Quiet Revolution." Lesage reversed the guiding philosophy of the previous governments in Quebec. He and his party increased government activity; the school system was secularized, hydro-electricity was nationalized and public administration was expanded and reformed.

Led by a new, entrepreneurial middle class, French-Canadian nationalism gave way to Quebec nationalism. These new Quebec nationalists saw that the use of the French language was declining in Canada and that Quebec's share of the Canadian population was dropping. Their response was to demand that they be *maîtres chez nous* (masters in our own house) in order to assure Quebec's role as guardian of French-Canadian civilization. They increased their pressure on the federal government throughout the 1960s, as they challenged Canada in judicial, social and political fields. Objections against federalism ranged from precise attacks on centralizing mechanisms such as the power of the federal government to disallow provincial legislation through to general claims that the *BNA Act* did not define a just federal system.

Modern Nationalism

While Quebec nationalism grew in the 1960s and 70s, at the federal level Prime Minister Pierre Elliott Trudeau, with his vision for French and English Canadians to be at home anywhere in the country, became the major spokesman for the more outward-looking style of nationalism.

In 1968 former provincial Cabinet minister René Lévesque left the Liberal Party and formed the Parti Québécois bringing Quebec nationalists together in a new party. In 1970 the extreme separatist Front de Libération du Québec (FLQ) initiated terrorist activities which culminated in the October Crisis of 1970, prompting the Trudeau government to invoke the *War Measures Act*. A British dipomat was kidnapped and a Quebec Minister was ultimately murdered. That same year, the Parti Québécois received 24% of the popular vote in its first provincial election.

By 1976, 41% of Quebec voters cast their ballots for the PQ with its platform of "good government" and a proposed referendum on sovereignty-association. The PQ won its first election. Within a short time the new government alarmed the business community and escalated tensions in French/English relations with Bill 101, the Charter of the French language in Quebec, which declared the intention to make the province unilingual. In order to make French the language of business it imposed French language requirements on businesses, made French the legal language for statutes and legal documents, required that all commercial signs and billboards be in French, and restricted access to English schools in the province.

The result of Lévesque's promised referendum on sovereignty-association, held in May 1980, was a blow to separatism. The population voted *non* — not to negotiate — by 60% to 40%. In other words, when they were asked if they wanted to be citizens of Quebec or Canada, Quebeckers chose Canada; they preferred Prime Minister Trudeau's promise of "renewed federalism" to even simple "discussions" that might lead to separatism.

The ground for the current constitutional crisis was laid in 1982 when, after long and difficult negotiations, the federal Liberal government of Pierre Trudeau patriated the Constitution from Great Britain. The compromise reached between nine of the ten provinces and the federal government excluded, isolated and angered Quebec's separatist government. The humiliated Quebec Premier, René Lévesque, informed his constitutents that they had been deserted: Canada, he said, had separated from Quebec. Trudeau reiterated an earlier promise to Quebec that their concerns would be met through a "renewed federalism."

Support for the PQ dwindled, and the party was defeated in 1985 by the Liberals led by Robert Bourassa. The nationalist challenge in Quebec was subdued by the improved state of the economy, a new entrepreneurial spirit, and Bourassa's successful dealings with Ottawa.

It was Premier Bourassa who formulated Quebec's interests after the 1982 constitutional patriation and negotiated their inclusion in the provincial Liberal Party's demands. It fell to Prime Minister Brian Mulroney to make good on the promise of renewed federalism. Quebec's lastest nationalist cycle was initiated by the inept handling of those demands by the Mulroney government.

Through a bungled procedure and flawed offer, the Meech Lake accord, Prime Minister Mulroney escalated and prolonged the constitutional crisis. By opening the cupboard to all comers he extended what was to be the "Quebec round" to a bargaining fest which brought new shopping lists from other provinces and societal groups, raising expectations which could not all be met.

After the rejection of Meech Lake, Quebec elites seethed about the treatment accorded their province. The basic question has been whether the province should push for greater powers within the Canadian federation or demand outright independence.

At what one might call the policy-makers' level over that question, Quebec split into four groups: the Independentists, who favour outright statehood for Quebec; the Sovereignists, who favour an increase in the degree of sovereignty for Quebec, but who do not necessarily wish to define sovereignty as meaning an absolute break from Canada; the Allairist Sovereignists, who favour the extreme decentralization of Canada in which very few powers would be left to the central government; and the Federalists, who favour the continued existence of Quebec within Canada, most of whom, however, wish the readjustment of federal/provincial powers, and favour at least the earlier five basic demands of the Quebec Liberal party and the consequent Meech Lake accord.

Public opinion polls in the 1990s show Quebeckers as a whole to be fairly evenly divided over the issue of independence. Sometimes they indicate the possibility of a vote in favour of independence, sometimes against. The context of the survey and the wording of the question determine the outcome. Clearly, however, support for independence is persistent, and if the Parti Québécois under the leadership of Jacques Parizeau were to be elected it could easily provoke a situation in which it could manipulate a referendum to suit its ends.

Jacques Parizeau argues that there must be a vote on sovereignty and claims that when his party is elected there will be independence for Quebec. The polls on party support in Quebec indicate a close race between the Liberals and the Parti Québécois. A March 1992 poll confirmed a stable trend line since the provincial election of 1989, with the Parti Québécois continuing to out poll the Liberals 49% to 44%.

French Separatists: Who They Are and What They Want

There are some realities that Canadians should keep in mind when confronting separatism from any quarter, especially from Quebec. First, Quebec does have the material resources to exist as a separate state. Second, it is not at all clear that independence is what the majority of Quebeckers want.

There is no doubt that Quebec could survive today as an independent state. Quebec's population of over six million, over 80% of whom are French-speaking, would tower above most of the states in the United Nations. In fact, an independent Quebec would have a population among the top one-third of such states and a geographical territory greater than 90% of them. This knowledge buttresses separatist arguments and feeds their nationalistic dreams. They ignore or minimize the fact that the standard of living of Quebec residents would fall for an indeterminate time after independence. Like Jello, these dreams aren't very solid, but they sell well.

The growth of separatism in Quebec is undisputed. If a graph of the votes for separatist parties were drawn it would indicate a clear trend in the direction of independence. The rise of opinion in favour of parties which favour separatism over the past few years has shown an average increase of about 1% a year. If this were accepted as a linear trend, there would be a vote for separatism about the year 2000.

Mainstream separatists prefer independence because, they say, both French and English will be free to "grow better." This is a difficult viewpoint for English-speaking Canadians to deal with and it sounds vaguely reminiscent of the apartheid rhetoric of South Africa. For these strong separatists there is no desire to compromise. It does not matter if English Canadians across this country like and appreciate Quebec and Quebeckers, or whether they are making efforts to become bilingual, or whether they admire French-Canadian culture. These niceties have nothing to do with the separatists' desire to be independent. This group simply wants Quebec francophones to be in total control of their own lives with no concessions or negotiations with anybody else. Their voices would be more important in their own small world and they are more secure there than as part of a larger, more diverse country.

This stand leaves no way for English-Canadians, or those with views counter to independence, to respond. In confrontation with this viewpoint, English-speaking Canadians would do well to remember that this is only one group of Québécois — albeit a very vocal one.

There is a strong element of ethnic pride, a feeling of "we-ness" among separatists that excludes all who are not born of French-Canadian stock. Pierre Trudeau, Mordecai Richler and others have mocked their tribalist appeal which is apparent as the political elite try to manipulate the masses. The kind of nationalism that is based on the tribal appeal to "those of pure stock" invites racism. As Mordecai Richler put it in an interview in *The Globe and Mail*, (March 10, 1992), "Québec au Québécois is a tribal cry. They don't want Anglos or Jews or Asians." Many Québécois are aware of the negative racial implications of this kind of appeal, but until recently few have spoken against it. When we ask separatists if *they* would set up a federal system to protect minorities within a separate Quebec they invariably reply no, they would not need to. That is a worrying response, particularly for minorities within Quebec's borders.

The Myth of Independence

The majority of Quebeckers do not want independence. Thomas D'Arcy McGee remarked during the Confederation debates in 1867 that those who were against Canada were only "concerned with their own insignificance." His comment captured the essence of the problem of state-building in a country as large and diverse as Canada. It is easy to champion local interests. It is much harder to work for the good of the whole, and to convince citizens to reduce or extinguish parochial interests for the good of the majority.

Today, the province of Quebec provides a major example of this problem. A few self-serving individuals and groups, seeking to aggrandize themselves and become bigger fish in a smaller pond, are currently taking advantage of a leadership vacuum and economic malaise in an attempt to destroy the country for their own ends. They are spreading myths and half truths.

Separatists such as Jacques Parizeau and Lucien Bouchard, leader of the Bloc Québécois, have romanticized the vision of a future, independent Quebec. They do not offer concrete examples of countries that provide a better quality of life for their citizens than Canada already does. Yet it should be incumbent on those who challenge Canada to be precise about exactly how the majority of citizens, and not just their particular small elite, would be better off by following their radical prescriptions.

Instead, fed by a school of nationalist historians who have virtually obliterated competing interpretations of Quebec history and traditions, separatist politicians conjure up sentiments of humiliation at the hands of *les Anglais* to justify their extremist demands. History, which should be a unifying force for Canadians, is used to produce strongly felt and deeply rooted feelings of injustice based much more on feeling than on fact.

Today, there is a solid core of just over a million Quebec separatists; they militate and vote for all separatist causes whether at the local, provincial or federal level. They will persist, no matter what constitutional concessions are made to Quebec by the federal government. And given separatist strength among the youth of the province their numbers may slowly continue to grow. English-speaking Canadians cannot be complacent about meeting the needs of francophone Quebec if they want Canada to remain united.

However, it is important to keep these one million plus separatists in perspective. They are very much a minority of French-speaking Quebeckers. Yet often, their rhetoric drowns out the voices of about five million others — many of whom really do not care much about the constitutional debate. What most aspire to is a job, security, a good life, and to remain in Canada. Studies have shown that francophones and anglophones share the same democratic and liberal values, the same concept of rights and freedoms, and the same range of opinions on the role of the state. Most want the incessant constitutional wrangling to stop.

Public opinion polls in the province of Quebec show incredible ambiguity in French-Canadian desires for federalism, sovereignty and independence. *L'actualité* polls, for example, show beyond a doubt that confusion and indecision reign on all questions about the future of the province. A CROP poll conducted in April 1992 found that 16% of Quebeckers were hard core Quebec nationalists; 22% were moderate Quebec nationalists; 26% were hard core Canadian nationalists; 18% were moderate Canadian nationalists; and 18% were very undecided. A cartoon which summarized the results of the polling on these questions about choosing Quebec or Canada showed a young boy saying essentially, "It's like having to choose between chocolate and ice cream for life...it's very hard when you like them both!"

English-speaking Canadians should keep in mind that French-speaking Quebeckers are now twice as likely to identify themselves as Québécois than as French-Canadian, and more than six times as likely to identify themselves as Québécois than as Canadians. At the same time, however, there is every indication that this identification is not mutually exclusive. According to McGill University sociologist Maurice Pinard, a significant majority of Quebec francophones — 62% in 1991 — feel profoundly attached to Canada. For this reason, most Québécois still prefer some form of renewed federalism over any other option.

Outside Quebec, Canadians watch separatist demonstrations on television, listen to M. Parizeau huff and puff in his mocking, pompous style about the inevitability of separation, and read stories about language police enforcing petty rules about whether the word "french fries" can appear on a hot dog stand in Gracefield. As when man bites dog, that makes news. Ordinary, everyday cordial relationships and friendships between English and French are never highlighted or discussed. English-speaking Canadians begin to feel that Quebec francophones are all of the same view, all nationalists with a grudge. They are not told that Quebec's language laws are not universally endorsed in that province, and, in fact, have been vigorously criticized by a number of prominent French-language publications and leaders.

Demographic trends show that the francophone presence outside Quebec will continue its steady decline. The percentage of Canadians with French as their mother tongue began to drop in 1951. At that time the French language group accounted for 29% of the total population, compared to about 25% in 1986. At that rate, by the year 2000, close to 95% of Canada's francophone population will live in Quebec.

Quebec, meanwhile, is expected to become gradually more francophone in composition. The 1986 census shows that the proportion of Quebec residents who speak French at home is slowly rising (83% in 1986). It also shows that non-francophone residents are learning French in increasing numbers; 54% of Quebec anglophones said they were bilingual, as did 47% of those whose mother tongue was neither English nor French.

On the other hand, the province's low birthrate indicates that its demographic weight within Canada could decline below its present 24% by the year 2000. Given present trends, Canadians must expect Quebec francophones to continue their struggle to preserve the pre-eminence of the French language and culture within their province.

These demographic concerns motivated the Quebec government to take steps to assert Quebec's distinctive character and create the now infamous language laws and "language police" which have done so much to discredit francophone Quebec in the eyes of other Canadians. The spiral of restrictive language laws began with an attempt to force Greek, Italian and Portuguese immigrants to have their children educated in French. In 1968, the Catholic school board of St-Léonard in suburban Montreal attempted to deny English education to its largely Italian population. The Quebec government introduced Bill 63 to mollify these parents and to allow parents in Quebec to educate their children in the language of their choice.

Nationalists were enraged. In 1974 Premier Bourassa responded by passing Bill 22 which said children of immigrants had to be enrolled in French schools, except for children who could demonstrate a sufficent knowledge of English. In 1977, under the new PQ government of René Lévesque, Bill 101, the *French Language Charter*, was introduced. It said that regardless of where a child came from — even from another province within Canada — he or she must be educated in French unless one of the parents had been to an English school in Quebec. Furthermore, any company with more than fifty employees must conduct all internal business in French. All English, or even bilingual, commercial signs would be illegal by 1981. And towns, rivers and mountains that bore English names were to be renamed in French.

Bill l0l directly contradicted the *Charter of Rights and Freedoms*. On this basis, the Quebec Association of Protestant School Boards brought a suit against the Government of Quebec. The Quebec Superior Court ruled on September 8, 1982, that the *Charter* took precedence over Bill l0l. This was immediately appealed by the government of Quebec. On December 22, 1986, the Quebec Court of Appeal ruled that the ban on languages other than French on commercial signs violated freedom of expression as protected by the Canadian, and also the Quebec, *Charter of Rights*. In a second ruling, it said that Quebec had the power to prevent the display of unilingual signs. Bourassa said the sign law could not be revoked until the Supreme Court of Canada had ruled on it.

In December 1988, nearly two years after the ruling of the Quebec Court of Appeal, the Supreme Court ruled on Section 58 of Bill l0l. It presented two court judgments: one was a challenge to Section 58 of Bill l0l by five businesses that questioned the rule that commercial sign laws in Quebec had to be in French only. The second was the case of Allan Singer dealing with the legality of English-only signs. In the first case the Supreme Court declared that the sign law was a violation of freedom of expression and stated that a ban on other languages was not needed to defend the French language. In the second case, the court ruled that the province was entitled to pass a law requiring the predominant display of the French language.

Almost immediately, Bourassa invoked the notwithstanding clause and then introduced Bill 178 in the National Assembly, banning English on outdoor signs, but allowing it and other languages on indoor signs, providing that French was predominant. Predictably, language wars within the province of Quebec escalated with ridiculous debates over size, colour and placement of letters on signs. Tolerance, as the basis of civilized society, was trampled.

Although the reasons for concern were real, such draconian measures against minority linguistic groups incited confrontation and hostility and appealed to the basest instincts of the ethnic majority in Quebec against its minorities and vice versa.

On Unilingualism or Bilingualism

Language is perhaps the most visible manifestation of the French-English fault line. Unilingualism in English Canada is a hysterical response to loud separatist voices which do not speak for all French Canadians, not even a majority of those who live in Quebec.

Defensive advocates of unilingualism prefer to segment Canadians into walled-off groups. They see culture in terms of black and white, winners and losers. According to their philosophy one must identify with English *or* French, not both. Affiliation with, or support for, one culture is all that is allowed. To embrace a second cultural group is to abandon the first.

It is a timorous, parochial stand that does not befit a multicultural society. And it is an inadequate and spiteful action against all French Canadians because of the separatist aspirations of a minority of them. As Dr. Victor Goldbloom said in his first report to Parliament as Commissioner of Official Languages in the spring of 1992: "A strong dose of tender loving care and a sedative would go a long way toward curing Canada's linguistic tensions."

Cultural affiliation should not be viewed in stark zero-sum terms. When English Canadians learn a second language they pass through a doorway to a new culture. They do not give up anything that is theirs, or become less English. They enrich their lives and build bonds of understanding and tolerance.

And tolerance must be the cornerstone of this country's strength. Without it the country will founder and disintegrate on the shoals of parochial division. Canadians should be clamouring for more, not fewer opportunities to understand different cultures and languages. They should be eager and proud to take advantage of the unique possibilities afforded by an aboriginal inheritance, two founding European peoples and a rich multi-cultural component.

In practical terms today that means extending a hand to minority francophone communities struggling to survive in a sea of anglophones. And *vice versa* for English in Quebec. Like winter, our historical cultural inheritance is one of the costs of being Canadian. But it is also one of our greatest assets. When charges of enforced bilingualism erupt they are usually based on misunderstandings, ignorance and a failure to appreciate the 200-year history of cooperation that has existed between French- and English-speaking Canadians.

Specific psychological elements serve to buttress a stable, democratic society. Research indicates that there must be a balance of attitudes that are active and passive, emotional and neutral toward the political system. There must be a balance in cleavage and consensus. And there must be diffuse social trust. When language is raised as a political issue by a municipality, as it was in Sault Ste. Marie which abruptly declared itself unilingual in the late 1980s, the action is harsh and corrosive and certain to deepen the already existing fault lines and break down social trust between groups.

Although it is the flag-tramplers and name-callers that get most of the media attention, there is plenty of good will in Canada. The population of Rosemere, a town just outside Montreal, showed in a referendum in the spring of 1992 that they wanted their town to be allowed to keep its bilingual status even though the anglophone population had shrunk considerably below the "legal limit" to remain bilingual according to Quebec language laws. The major issued a statement to the effect that the francophone population owed a great debt to the anglophones who had built such a wonderful town in a spirit of tolerance, and it would be unfair to treat the anglophones worse just because they were no longer the majority. They exposed the French language law "as an ass," and reaffirmed the spirit of toleration and good will that has been the dominant trademark of Canadian society.

Leadership is needed to nourish national policies such as bilingualism which bridge the fault lines of the country. Leadership, for example, could destroy the myth that bilingualism is too onerous by reiterating the basic truth that the requirements of the Official Languages Act are extremely modest. Bilingualism does not mean that everyone must speak English and French. It means that all Canadians can communicate with their governments in the official language of their choice. Claims that have been made by Premier Don Getty and others that official bilingualism is a punitive and expensive failure would be instantly recognized as foolish if federal leaders kept some important facts before the population. In his own province of Alberta, for example, of 13,000 federal civil servants only 400 (about 3%) are required to be bilingual. The other 97% are unilingual anglophones. The francophone population of Alberta is just over 2%. Is this what Mr. Getty laments as the "heavy burden of enforced bilingualism?"

Across the four western provinces 3.4% of government jobs are designated bilingual. Francophones represent 2.2% of the population. The match is appropriate and just. In fact, the only place where bilingual employment and the composition of citizens is not closely related is in Quebec outside the National Capital region. There a huge disparity exists between bilingual positions and linguistic origins — in favour of anglophones. In Quebec City the anglophone population is 2.2%, but the designated bilingual positions are 41.8% of the total. Most bilingual positions, of course, are in Ottawa where half of the jobs are earmarked. But that does not mean that francophones are hogging more than their fair share of the jobs. There are bilingual anglophones too. The representation of francophones in the upper levels of the civil service is very close to their percentage of the national population.

The gripe that the cost of providing federal services in both official languages is impoverishing Canadians as a whole should also be dispelled as a short-sighted myth. That cost is only one-third of one percent of the total federal budget of over $150 billion. This is hardly an outrageous amount to pay in order to treat fellow Canadians courteously, with dignity and with respect.

In spite of these facts, the myth has spread in anglophone communities that bilingualism is unfair and being "pushed down our throats." Where are the politicians who have been dispelling the myths? Where are the party leaders on this topic? Are they too busy pandering to special interests in order to win their votes? Not since the passage of the 1969 Official Languages Act has the federal government conducted a national publicity campaign to explain the policy of official bilingualism. This has been a gross dereliction of leadership. Political leaders spend money to get themselves elected, but not to destroy the myths that threaten national unity.

There are corresponding myths among Québécois that should be dispelled. Separatists encourage the myth that French-Canadians have no voice in Ottawa, that Ottawa does not represent Quebec's interests. This is absurd. Since 1968 Canada has had a Prime Minister from Quebec for all but about a year and a half. Quebec is always well represented in federal cabinets. Senior government posts rotate between French- and English-speakers. Although Francophones still hold slightly less than their statistical share of jobs in the civil service, they are certainly not discriminated against in Ottawa.

More Solitudes? Other Ethnic Divisions

Forgotten in most constitutional debates is the simple fact that Canada consists of many people who are of neither French nor English extraction. Today, about 40% of Canadians are neither English nor French. Within the next 20 or 30 years these so-called "other ethnics" could constitute a majority of Canada's population.

Over 100 ethnic groups have been identified in Canada, the largest being German (5%), Italian (4%), Ukrainian (2%) and native peoples (2%). These ethnic groups are very unevenly mixed throughout the population. According to the last census, about 16% of the Canadian population is foreign-born, and more than half of that number lives in five large cities: Toronto, Montreal, Vancouver, Edmonton and Winnipeg.

In recognition of the burgeoning numbers of immigrants of non-English or French extraction, the federal government in 1971 defined Canada as being multicultural within a bilingual English-French framework. Since that time, services on which ethnic groups could draw have steadily increased. The current policy of the federal government is to promote the retention of characteristic cultural features of ethnic groups which wish to maintain their identities.

With the current low birthrate of 1.7 children per family and an aging population (by the year 2013 one in every four Canadians will be 65 or older), Canada needs to accept significantly more immigrants than it did up to 1988 in order to curb the population decline. Since the pattern of immigrant sources has changed dramatically in the last decade, Canadians must anticipate a greater racial mix in the population than ever before.

Visible Minorities

Over the next decade, the number of Canadians who are members of visible minorities is projected to more than double. A recent study by Professor T. John Samuel concludes that the current 2.5 million Canadians who are members of a visible minority will rise to 5.7 million by 2001. That would represent an increase from 9.6% currently to 17.7% of the total population. In large metropolitan areas the percentage would be even higher: 56% in Toronto; 39% in Vancouver; and 25% in Edmonton and Calgary, for example. Ontario will be the home of the largest number of visible minorities by 2001, followed by BC, Quebec, Alberta and Manitoba. The composition of

Canada's visible minorities, the Samuel study says, will be relatively unchanged; it will remain approximately 23% Chinese, 19% south Asians, 19% blacks, 13% West Asians or Arabs, 8% Filipinos and 6% Latin Americans.

Perhaps the most important economic message from the Samuel study comes in the conclusion that the visible minorities will be relatively more affluent than many Canadians. They will control about 20% of the country's gross domestic product because they tend to be better educated than average Canadians and live in urban areas where incomes are higher. It is imperative that society be prepared for this enormous change if Canada is to avoid the kind of racial tensions that have become the trademark of many American cities. Strong leadership will be needed to look ahead and introduce ways to ease tensions between racial groups.

Some English and French Canadians fear that their significance as members of founding nations will be undermined by the growing numbers of other-ethnics. Other people argue that multiculturalism fragments Canadian society. There is, however, no evidence that either of these arguments is valid. To date, Canadian society has proven remarkably resilient in accommodating large numbers of immigrants with relatively little social stress. Since World War II, only Australia and Israel have accepted comparable numbers of immigrants in proportion to their populations. Inevitably, a rapid influx of immigrants into urban areas results in competition for housing, jobs and social facilities. Nonetheless, positive attitudes toward multiculturalism have been shown to be strongest in areas where "other" ethnic groups are most concentrated.

Canada has become a pluralist society. Tolerance toward people of different cultural and ethnic backgrounds is a necessity. And this maturity can only come from understanding, not building walls around, minorities. Social science research has proven that people with more than one cultural background are more tolerant of others. Knowledge about, and appreciation of, other groups is an enriching experience that encourages individuals to feel better toward their country. Having two of the world's most useful official languages is not a negative, but a positive attribute, a wonderful opportunity and gift.

Native Peoples

A second rapidly deteriorating fault line lies between Canada's native peoples — the aboriginals who consist of Inuit and status and non-status Indians, including Métis — and other Canadians. While the British authorities made many efforts to accommodate the French minority in the 19th century, they demonstrated little such concern for the rights of the "First Nations." Successive colonial and Dominion governments deprived them of their land (by means fair or foul), herding them into reserves and subjecting them to the draconian Indian Acts.

The first law concerning native peoples was vague and not yet indicative of the shabby way they were to be treated later. The *Royal Proclamation* of 1763 recognized the land rights of Indians and described a rough "Proclamation Line" dividing hunting grounds from land that could be settled by Europeans. It did not state, however, the exact western or eastern extent of these reserved lands. Further laws to protect Indian lands were enacted in Upper and Lower Canada and in Nova Scotia, New Brunswick, Prince Edward Island and British Columbia.

Just who was an "Indian" was not legally defined until the first *Indian Act* in 1876. However, the concept of "status Indians" was adopted in order to determine who had rights to Indian land. Status Indians were divided into 2 groups: treaty Indians who "took treaty" with the Crown, surrendering land rights for specific benefits, and registered Indians who did not. Both types of status Indians received benefits and privileges from the federal government. Non-status Indians were all others of Indian ancestry who, one way or another, had actively or passively given up their status rights but not their Indian identity. Métis, for example, are descendants of unions between Indians and whites who kept their Indian identity but did not enjoy special status under federal policy. These distinctions remain today.

Once Confederation took place the role of native peoples in Canada took a sharp downward turn. In 1867 the federal Parliament was assigned legislative jurisdiction over Indians and reserve lands (*BNA Act* 19:24). Two years later, legislation was passed reflecting a clear policy of assimilation of aboriginal peoples. Essentially, Indians on reserves were to be protected temporarily until they learned European methods of farming. They would then be qualified to relinquish their Indian status. Reserve privileges were considered as a kind of probationary period of Canadian citizenship.

Then, in 1876, the first *Indian Act* was enacted. This Act was amended frequently in subsequent years, but always with the aim of suppressing Indian traditions and extending government control over status Indians on reserves. The current Act, passed in 1951, remains an essentially 19th century statute which reflects early biases and intent.

Court decisions over the years have been unable to adequately define and recognize aboriginal rights. However, until the *Constitution Act 1982*, Parliament had the power to pass laws extinguishing any or all such rights. Native groups never agreed that Parliament had such sweeping powers as they claimed. The *Constitution Act 1982* recognizes aboriginal and treaty rights, and provides a new basis for court challenges.

Native peoples still occupy a dependent, semi-colonial position in regard to the federal and provincial governments. Government proposals to end Indian status and repeal the Indian Act have been strongly criticized by natives who want greater recognition of their traditional rights, settlement of land claims, and power to manage their own lands and affairs.

Métis and non-status Indians, too, find themselves largely among the under-privileged sections of Canadian society and are subject to similar racial stereotyping and prejudice. The Inuit, because of their location in the Northwest Territories, northern Quebec and Labrador, were largely by-passed in the economic and political modernization of Canada. There are just over 25,000 Inuit in Canada, scattered throughout the Arctic in eight tribal groups. They have never been subject to the *Indian Act* and were largely ignored by government until 1939 when they officially became a federal responsibility. Since that time they have been classified as "Indians" for the purposes of the Constitution.

Native peoples are the most politically conscious visible minority today. As a whole, unlike many other minorities, Canada's native peoples are economically deprived. Many are plagued by alcoholism and depression as they strive to cope with the loss of their traditional lifestyle because of the encroachments of modern society and environmental disasters.

The treatment of native peoples is a point of shame for Canadians. The handling of status Indians who live on reserves is indicative of the problem. In modern times this population has grown substantially, largely because of reductions in infant mortality rates and high rates of fertility. Their rate of population growth is well over twice that of the rest of Canadians. Approximately 40% of the Indian population is between the ages of 15 and 35, compared to 35% of the total Canadian population. In 1988 the number of registered Indians was an estimated 530,384, of whom 273,766 were located in Indian communities or on Crown land. They are distributed in 633 bands.

During the post-Second-World-War period, Indian migration to the cities increased dramatically due to poor conditions on the reserves. This increased pockets of ghettoization in cities where the migrants suffered from the same type of conditions as on reserves—namely high unemployment and economic deprivation.

The *Indian Act* was intended to protect native peoples within Canadian society and to provide a broad range of social programs. All Indians receive the same benefits as other Canadians, such as family allowances and pensions, and status Indians also have a right to a wide variety of other benefits in the field of education, health care and housing. They have been left in a state of dependency on government.

Despite (some would say because of) this government assistance, many Indians live in abysmal social conditions. Examples of these conditions can be summarized as follows:

- High school completion rates are low: 20% compared with about 70% for non-natives.
- Only 22% of the adult population has training beyond high school compared to 40% of the rest of the Canadian population.
- Participation in the labour force is low: 50% compared to 65% for non-natives.
- Unemployment is about twice as high as the national average.
- Employment pay is about 2/3 the national average.
- Life expectancy, infant mortality, suicide and violent death are all worse for natives than non-natives.
- Native children are four times more likely to die by the age of 14 than non-natives.
- Deaths by fire on reserves are six times that of the Canadian population.
- Environmental hazards threaten traditional ways of life: industrial and resource development have polluted waterways and disrupted fish and game stocks upon which many depend for food and livelihood.
- Reserves endure low housing standard, with overcrowding and insufficient access to indoor plumbing, running water and electricity as the norm.

Undoing the Past

While they are divided on many issues, the native peoples are united in a quest for settlement of their land claims and recognition of their "inherent right of self-government." Their demands on Canadian society are made through several groups, the most important of which include the Assembly of First Nations, the Native Council of Canada, the Inuit National Body, the Inuit Tapirisat of Canada, and the Métis National Council.

Land claims are an urgent problem. Current reserves are generally inadequate for the economic development and resource needs of the aboriginal communities which live on them. In order to become economically self-sufficient, they must be assured of a secure and expanded land base. The alternative is to remain dependent on governments and for increasing numbers of aboriginal groups to seek court settlements over disputes in such matters as logging and mining on Crown lands licenced by the provincial government.

About half the 633 status Indian bands of Canada have not ceded their traditional territories by treaty with the Canadian government. The Indians of most of British Columbia, Quebec and the territories have not entered into such treaties, and claim outstanding aboriginal rights over, and title to, their traditional lands.

The current land claims process is notoriously complicated and slow because of limited government resources: only six claims across the country are in negotiation at any one time. All other groups must wait until those negotiations are completed and each case takes about 20 years to settle. At this rate injustices will drag on and claims will still be being heard well into the next century.

Apart from a few settlements in Alberta and Manitoba, Métis and non-status Indians do not have reserves at all. In fact the exact size of these populations is not even know. A very rough and conservative estimate is that there are three Métis and non-status Indians for every registered Indian. They are thinly scattered across the country and do not benefit from the special provisions for reserves and services under the *Indian Act.*

One further complication to the issue of territorial claims is that, according to the Assembly of First Nations which represents Status Indians, Quebec's Indians do not want to be part of the province if it decides to separate from Canada. An Assembly's Report on the Constitution states: "If Quebec has the right to separate from Canada, First Nations have the right to make their own decisions. And if that means separation from Quebec, so be it." The Cree claim more than a million square kilometers of sparsely populated land, a tract bigger than Ontario and nearly twice the size of France. It includes the land on which the James Bay power installations are located, which generates nearly half of Quebec's current electricity, as well as the vast untapped hydro potential of other northern rivers. This could be the most explosive issue raised by Quebec independence.

The second broad, contentious issue concerning native peoples concerns their demand for the right to "self-government" being included in the Constitution. According to their leadership such rights should not be defined in the documents because they are "inherent rights" which the native peoples have never given up in past treaties.

Public opinion polls indicate strong support for native self-government, although it appears that neither the Canadian public nor native groups themselves have any clear idea what exactly is meant by the term. Reid polls in December 1991 found public opinion evenly divided between unconditional support, qualified support and outright opposition to native self-government, with the level of support increasing the further away people lived from native peoples and the less they knew about them. The respondents were also very confused about the issues. When pressed about the details of self-government they were very conservative. They equated self-government with municipal government, which is not what native peoples themselves have in mind.

Self-government has a nice ring to it, and Canadians are very ashamed of how aboriginals have been treated in this country. However, the concept of self-government may not be so full of charm when it is spelled out.

For years, native peoples have argued that no Canadian government is in a position to grant a right which predates it and which has no source in any imperial, colonial or Dominion authority. They consider that their right to govern themselves is a preexisting, continuing, natural right given to them by the Great Creator. It cannot be given or taken away by any government. They reason that they have never themselves given up their right to self-government, and it has never been extinguished by any legislation (because such power could not exist), as it is not the gift of any Canadian government.

The claims to self-government would not have been entertained by any federal government in Canada a few years ago, but suddenly, in the early 1990 constitutional negotiations, the concept of "inherent rights" became acceptable to many political leaders eager for any agreement. The federal leadership, in particular, has been wishy-washy enough to accept anything in order to get a deal, and most provincial leaders by and large are not worried because they think the federal government will pick up the tab for whatever is conceded in negotiations.

There is no doubt that some form of aboriginal self-government is required, but the issue needs to be clarified. Women, for example, comprise 52% of the native population. They demand that the gender equality clauses of the *Charter of Rights and Freedoms* continue to apply to them after self-government is accorded. When government officials tried to define and circumscribe the powers of native self-government to include *Charter* protection, the leader of the Assembly of First Nations, Ovide Mercredi, commented: "Our perspective is that you've taken our land, you've taken our resources, you've taken our language, you've taken our pride... what is there left... to take from us? Our political will? Well, [you] cannot have it."

Lack of government leadership concerning this vitally important fault line is bound to increase misunderstandings between native peoples and their fellow Canadians. In the rush to piece together a constitutional agreement and preserve their credibility at the polls in the upcoming election, the federal government made rash concessions and avoided telling the truth about what native self-government means for Canada. Perhaps this point will be addressed by the Royal Commission on Aboriginal Peoples that was set up in April 1992 to deal with issues affecting Indians, Métis and Inuit ranging from self-government and land claims to education and justice. Hopefully, it will produce some specific and realistic solutions to the obvious (and not so obvious) problems.

REGIONAL FAULT LINES

Regionalism is not a uniquely Canadian problem. Regional boundaries, based on different political cultures and economies, are a fact of life in most countries. People develop an emotional identification with, or attachment to, a given territory. This is manifested in specific interests—cultural, economic and political—which are defined and articulated for a particular area.

Regionalist demands are not inherently nationalistic; they do not usually call for the development of a new state as is now the case with Quebec. Regionalist leaders demand only changes in the economic and political arrangements between the region and central governments of an extant state. Such political pressures emerge both from poorer regions which demand a greater share of the country's wealth and from richer provinces seeking to protect or even enhance their superior position.

In Canada regionalism has been a persistent factor in politics. Both the vast size of the country and the uneven economic development of the regions have meant that provinces have separate interests to protect and advance. Thus, the country is divided, for example, into regions based on oil-producing versus oil-consuming provinces, and richer versus poor regions. Even the federal form of government itself provides a structural guarantee to regionalism; indeed it was chosen partly because it would allow regional diversity.

Western Alienation

Along with urgent constitutional demands from Quebec, Canada is facing particularly strong demands from alienated regions, particularly the western provinces. Most recently, Alberta took the lead to exploit its leverage during the so-called "Canada round" of constitutional negotiations to win extra political clout for the West.

The broadest perception of Canada's national needs has been built around two founding peoples because of historical relationships between French and English Canadians. This is not, however, the western or regional vision of Canada. Largely because of the "melting-pot" mix of cultures and relatively few francophones in that region, the western vision is based more on economic development than cultural protection for minority language interests. Because it does not embrace the dual cultural view of Canada, westerners believe that their vision of the country is rejected and deemed illegitimate. According to western political scientists the western vision is largely ahistorical; since the population is ethnically varied and relatively new to the West, the people do not state their interests in terms of the early history of central and eastern Canada.

Throughout the West's history there has been a strong belief that the resource-rich prairie provinces were exploited by federal government policies which represented central Canadian interests. Issues of contention centred on federal freight-rate and tariff policies, which were held responsible for making the West a captive market for higher-priced manufactured goods from central Canada. These policies concomitantly increased the cost of exporting products from the West. Thus it is argued that such policies have allowed the East to remain the industrial heartland of Canada while the West has been forced to carry a disproportionate share of the costs.

The most salient of these policy issues today is the National Energy Program of 1980. During the world energy crisis of the 1970s, the Liberal government of Pierre Trudeau attempted to combat the rising costs of oil and gas by legislation and programs which effectively prevented the West from reaping the market price for their resources. Western frustration grew as it was realized that the NEP would in effect prevent western provinces from improving their financial position in the country. Some car stickers from the West read—"Let the Eastern bastards freeze in the dark." Those in the East were apt to say "Down with the blue-eyed Sheiks."

Economic issues concerning resources and taxation which arise periodically between western and central Canada are interpreted within the western vision of the country and become manifested in constitutional disputes. In the 1970s, western criticism of the political and economic dominance of central Canada began to be expressed in a desire for constitutional reform. During 1975–1981, the western provincial governments refused to compromise over patriation of the Constitution from Britain unless the federal government would reduce its power, especially on economic issues. As a compromise, federal equalization payments to the provinces were enshrined in the 1982 constitutional package, as well as more provincial power over their own natural resources.

Western separatism flared briefly in the early 1980s, ignited by the re-election of the federal Liberal Party in 1980. Since the Liberals captured no seats west of Manitoba, the election resulted in the political disenfranchisement of western Canada. Frustrated by a lack of political power within the federal government, Westerners felt powerless against "centralist" policies, including bilingualism, metrication and immigration. There was a fear that the national government would drain the West of its wealth and leave it both economically and politically impoverished.

When the newly elected federal Liberal government initiated two aggressive federal policies the frustration exploded. Those policies were unilateral patriation of the Constitution and implementation of the National Energy Program, which many Westerners perceived as an attempt to rob them of their resource wealth.

The most significant public expression of western alienation was the formation in the early 1980s of various groups and political parties dedicated to the separation of the western provinces of Manitoba, Saskatchewan, Alberta, British Columbia, and, possibly, the Northwest Territories and Yukon from Canada. The two leading separatist groups in that period were the Western Canadian Federation (West-Fed) and the Western Canada Concept (WCC).

In a very short time, however, the popularity of western separatism dissipated and it never formed a permanent political movement. The groups had provided an outlet for frustration, but there was little agreement among them about what strategy to follow. A survey of the four western provinces in October 1980 showed that about 35% of the population thought the West was ignored in federal political decision-making. About 61% felt that the federal government discriminated against the West in economic terms. At the same time, however, 90% of westerners said they would prefer to remain part of Canada, even though 60% believed the West had sufficient resources to thrive on its own, indicating an essentially regionalist perspective and not a nationalist challenge to the Canadian state.

Feelings of alienation decreased after the decline of world oil prices. With the Conservative's 1984 electoral victory the western separatists thought they would obtain strong and effective western representation in government, and to some extent this expectation was valid; Mulroney's government dismantled the National Energy Program and the Trudeau marketing restrictions on the sale of oil and natural gas.

However, the feeling that the federal political system was stacked against the West persisted. In the 1988 general election a new protest movement called the Reform Party, headed by Preston Manning, conducted a credible campaign on behalf of western interests. Its demands for free trade and Senate reform found a ready audience among small-c conservative voters. It did not win any seats, but it obtained 15% of the votes in Alberta and affected Conservative and NDP electoral competition throughout the West.

All economic issues dividing western and central Canada continue to be interpreted within this context of alienation and the western conception that they are controlled by the great majority in the East.

Tyranny of the Majority

History helps to shape a civic identity by teaching citizens where they came from and where they stand in relation to others. However, in countries with deep regional divisions each area teaches history from its own, unique perspective; the same facts are seen differently and awarded different emphasis depending on the region concerned. If this tendency is not counterbalanced by a unifying mythology and common goals, it becomes a source of weakness, a flaw in the unifying fabric of the country.

This is a serious problem in Canada. In Quebec and Ontario, for example, reading Canadian history is like reading about two different countries. Western Canada, too, has its unique focus on events such as the construction of the railway, the displacement of native and Métis peoples and the wagon-loads of European and American immigrants who set up homesteads there. The unique regional perspectives are not complemented by a unifying mythology that all regions share. When political issues arise in the country they are perceived from totally different perspectives rather than one based on one people, one country.

However, regional discontent may be more a fabrication of elites than a strong feeling of the mass public. It is often to the benefit of the local political elite to exacerbate differences between provinces or regions and the federal government. Provincial premiers often play on regional sentiments to gain support in striking tough financial bargains with the federal government.

This is particularly true in the West where politicians nourish the view that Westerners are governed under the tyranny of a majority. The underlying problem is easily stated, but not easily resolved. The population of two provinces, Ontario and Quebec, considerably exceeds 50% of the entire country. Because of this fact, the outer regions generally perceive that the federal parliamentary system only represents central Canada, and therefore, to an extent, is merely a regional government for citizens in that part of the country. Many solutions to alienation have been proposed over the years by Westerners: switch political parties; abolish parties; electoral reform; Senate reform; abolish party discipline, and so on. The landscape is littered with reform initiatives. Westerners have agreed only on a goal — a more effective voice at the centre — but not how to achieve it.

It is tendentious to characterize the concerns of the West as one monolithic viewpoint. But the gravamen impacting on constitutional discussions emanates from two principles:

1. Each province should be regarded as equal and therefore anything that Quebec or Ontario obtains, each western province should get too.

2. There is a persistent view, especially from Alberta, that a Triple-E Senate — one that is elected, equal and effective — should be part of any constitutional package. During the 1992 constitutional negotiations Alberta, backed by Saskatchewan, Manitoba and Newfoundland, insisted that this meant that each province must have exactly the same number of Senators regardless of its population base.

The flaw in the Triple-E proposal is that it contradicts the basic democratic proposition of representation by population that has been present since Confederation. The equality of the vote is sacred. Representation, in this view, should be based on population, not wealth, property, tradition, region, or any other such factors. While western Canadians want a strong, effective upper house, central Canadians are adamant about the need to have a lower house which can be effective and not constantly be blocked by minority provincial representation in the Senate.

Senate reform has, however, become the focal point and rallying cry of the western provinces to redress the imbalance and ameliorate the slight that westerners feel. Triple-E has taken on a symbolism of its own that is even more important than the reality of change. Its advocates believe that election to the Senate would give Senators legitimacy; effectiveness would give them a strong voice vis-à-vis the lower house; equality would assure the West and the Atlantic provinces of a voice as strong as that of Ontario or Quebec.

As with other fault lines, regionalism in Canada is a permanent fact of life. But living with it on a daily basis does not mean that it can be ignored, or worse yet, that it should be used by politicians to score political points. Regional economic disparities are a fact of life in Canada. Since Confederation, the belief that the rich provinces and regions should help the poorer ones has been a fundamental part of the Canadian political culture. Sharing through economic redistribution is built into the political system and is viewed by Canadians as the fair way to cope with regional disparities. The uneven economic development of the provinces is to some extent compensated for by equalization payments, and provincial jostling for a fair share of the economic pie takes place within this basic redistribution framework.

The most extreme western view of the country has been expressed by two Calgary professors. In *Deconfederation: Canada Without Quebec*, David J. Bercuson and Barry Cooper declare categorically that Canada would be better off if Quebec were to separate from the country. Citing facts to support western alienation, and adopting western myths about the Constitution, they advocate an English-speaking country from coast to coast, minus Quebec. Their contention and policy prescription is, unwisely, taken seriously in many parts of the prairies, especially southern Alberta.

BRIDGING THE GAPS

The Double Standard of Self-Determination

The fault lines based on ethnicity, provincialism and regionalism often manifest themselves in demands for self-determination for regions, provinces or groups.

The very idea of self-determination generates deep emotion and unbridled energy. Political groups which seek to separate from larger state units in order to control their own destiny are spurred on by exhilaration, pride and a sense of group solidarity and belonging. Around the world, self-determination is viewed as a worthy principle, one which has been used to structure many states today. It has provided the rationale to end colonialism and free oppressed people in Africa, Asia, and throughout the world.

Most Canadians, too, believe that peoples, nations and races should be able to determine their own governments. But what are the rules and what are the limits of self-determination? For whom is separatism an acceptable expression of freedom and democracy, and for whom is it not? Principle and practice are often far apart. There is considerable bunkum about the issue. Canadians often support the principle and deny the practice — except, of course, when it concerns their own interests.

There is a virulent side-effect to self-determination which often infects groups seeking to separate. Fragmented states often become intolerant, coercive and oppressive toward other minorities in their midst. They create internal instability and economic turmoil and increase the likelihood of civil and external wars. The spectre of civil war in Yugoslavia has been a daily reminder of the ugly extreme of self-determination.

Around the world there are many groups, tribes, races and even nations which would like to become states — to have their own governments and determine their own future. But although the United Nations endorses the principle of self-determination, it clearly does not support this action for all of them.

Political leaders give lip service to the principle of self-determination, but when actually confronted with it they are often opposed, sometimes out of self-interest, sometimes because of a fear that it could create more and even greater injustice.

The idea of self-determination is likened to the concept of nationality. The notion that state boundaries should coincide with those of national communities is quite recent, dating approximately from the French Revolution. The idea that the state and nation are one persists today in principle, but is far from reality. In fact, it is difficult to name more than a handful of countries which do not contain more than one important ethnic group.

In Canada, the concept of self-determination receives unspoken acceptance — it is an idea that everybody seems to share but which is rarely articulated. Does Quebec have the right to determine its own future? Political leaders in Quebec and Ottawa unanimously share an implicit acceptance of that principle.

Only time will tell how deeply this belief is founded. It is uncertain how ordinary Canadians would act if ever confronted with the actual division of their country. In Quebec, Jacques Parizeau, leader of the Parti Québécois, upholds the principle of self-determination for Quebec but would deny it to minorities within the province. But if the principle of self-determination means the right of peoples, races and nations to pilot their own affairs, then certainly the practice must extend to native peoples and anglophones who may not wish to be part of a new Quebec state.

It is clear that the principles of self-determination need clarification. Too often Canadian political leaders adhere more to the principle of self-interest than to that of self-determination. Nowhere is this more evident than in the Parti Québécois.

Canada is More than its Parts

Acadian novelist Antonine Maillet was once asked, after she had been awarded the prestigious Goncourt Prize for Literature, how she regarded herself — as French, French-Canadian, Acadian, French-Acadian or Canadian. She replied that she was all of them in different proportions. It was an honest and direct response which reveals a great deal about how attachments to regions or ethnic groups do not make one any less "Canadian." She affirmed with pride the influence of the various cultural elements that were all a part of her life.

This idea, embraced by previous generations, that Canada is an interwoven tapestry — rather than a "melting-pot" — of various ethnic and regional backgrounds, cultures and interests is being unravelled in the creeping and insidious ideology of difference. Instead of concentrating on the whole tapestry this ideology focuses on particular sections. By doing so it neglects the tapestry itself, and what an important contribution each part makes to the strength and beauty of the whole.

There are valid ethnic and regional concerns which must be accommodated in Canadian society, but the key ingredient in smoothing over these differences is tolerance. Tolerance has been a key characteristic of Canadian society and has made it a world class country.

Canadians must be prepared to reach out and, when necessary, accept certain personal or financial costs for the good of the whole. Like Antonine Maillet, many Canadians are French, Acadian and Canadian at the same time or Italian, Italian-Canadian and Canadian — or any number of other variations from our cultural mosaic. They come from visible and non-visible groups. The culture is layered and interwoven like the strands of a tapestry, with different colours and textures complementing and extending each other.

Surely cultural and linguistic tolerance should be at the heart of that elusive cultural identity for which Canadians are always searching. This is a truer image of what Canada is and should be than the paranoid, selfish, "any gain for you is a loss for me" notion being expressed in many quarters today.

As a nation of immigrants Canada has a better-than-average track record of tolerance toward people of different races and cultures. But the escalation of ethnic tensions in recent years is foreboding. As immigration brings more visible minorities into the country, the reputation for tolerance is being tested.

In times of economic stress it takes very little to cause a society to turn on its visible and language minorities as scapegoats. The racism that is on the rise in a great many countries is also growing in Canada. The copy-cat rioting in downtown Toronto following the much more serious riot in Los Angeles in the spring of 1992 is indicative of tensions that are building. Current manifestations of racial prejudice are fed by hard economic times, large flows of immigration, and prejudice fed by nationalism. Except in Quebec, ethnicity and provincial borders do not coincide to any significant extent, and this has helped to diffuse problems, but the need for federal leadership and creative public policy is urgent.

Tolerance is a willingness to allow and even encourage nations and cultural groups to flourish within the state. Canadians have built a country on the premise that differences can make our Canadian nation stronger and more perfect. To survive and prosper that philosophy should be guarded and nourished.

On the surface Canadians, and especially their leaders, often overstate their regional, provincial or ethnic differences, outlining their specific grievances in the corrosive terms of independence, alienation and the need for self-government. When observers see that happening they should apply the scratch test. Canadians should be asked not where they are from or what their grievances are; instead they should be asked whether or not they are Americans. Almost invariably they will bristle and say of course they are Canadians. The majority, including Westerners, native peoples and Quebeckers, love their country and really do see themselves, and the various ethnic and regional identities which are important to them, as part of the whole, colourful tapestry — as part of Canada.

But a frayed and divided social fabric, flawed institutions and inept leadership on constitutional reform have exacerbated, instead of resolving, latent problems in the fields of French-English relations, aboriginal injustices and regional alienation. Bickering stand-offs between these groups prevent Canadians from focusing on more significant questions.

Who stands up for Canada as a whole? Normally it would be our leaders in the central institutions of government, but in Canada today serious flaws in those institutions and weak political leadership are preventing that from happening. It is up to Canadians themselves to take on that task.

3 Flaws in the Political Institutions: Constitution, Government and Parliament

"A dynamic state should not fear to reassess its political philosophy. That an agreement worked out a hundred years ago does not necessarily meet all the needs of the present should not necessarily be surprising."

— HRH Elizabeth II, (Address, Legislative Council, Quebec City, October 10, 1964)

The persistent ethnic and regional differences which cut across the Canadian landscape should be accommodated in ways which will strengthen, not weaken, the country as a whole. The challenge is to build governmental institutions which can bridge societal fault lines, promoting harmony and unity. Canada's hybrid government, based on the British parliamentary-cabinet system combined with federalism, has been moderately successful in this respect. But politics is never static, and constitutions are like living organisms. Problems which arise regularly in our Constitution and in the operation of government and Parliament must be recognized and resolved. When they are not, they aggravate ethnic discontent and invite public cynicism.

However, as Canadians today are only too well aware, reforming a constitution and governmental institutions is no simple matter. Winston Churchill once observed that those who enjoy sausage and respect democracy should not observe the making of either. The same might be said of constitutional reform. Vested interests make innovation difficult, even in times of strong federal leadership. A search for appropriate reforms has preoccupied the government and the Canadian public for years. It has been divisive and fruitless.

We have noted that three conditions are drawing the country toward weak, stalemated government. In the last chapter we looked at the first of them: the vision that the country is no more than a combination of ethnic, regional and other special interests. In this chapter, we consider the second condition: flawed political institutions — fractured federalism, prime ministerial dominance, and a weak legislature. In the next chapter, we consider leadership in Canadian history and assess the public's lack of confidence in institutions and leaders.

The combination of these three conditions — a vision of the country as nothing but special interests, flawed political institutions, and weak leadership — is creating the extreme public cynicism in Canada today. And, as we shall see, cynicism, combined with other factors which are already present in Canada, could be the last straw, the determining factor that causes the country to head toward disintegration.

The basic issues of contention about Canadian institutions and politics always come back to that eternal Canadian question: Which representatives, federal or provincial, get or keep what share of the public purse and power? The complexity and scope of this problem requires some background knowledge of the evolution of the Canadian Constitution and the federal structure as it exists today.

CONSTITUTIONAL CONFUSION

The constitution of a country describes its basic legal and political system. It outlines how government will function and what it may or may not do. It delineates how power is distributed in society and provides the legitimacy for leaders to act authoritatively. If the political system is to remain stable, the basic rules of politics need to be structured so as to reduce tensions and problems which emerge along the basic fault lines or weaknesses in the composition of the country.

Canadians need to understand and appreciate today's Constitution before they reform it. There *are* problems with the Constitution as it exists; however, they are not as vast as political leaders pretend. The basic difficulties can be blamed on a weakening federal system and a too-powerful Prime Minister and executive. Federally, political power has gravitated from the many to the few. Partly in response to this, provincial leaders want to decentralize power to the detriment of federal authority.

In order to solve the current problems of our fractured federal system some, but not many, gradual adjustments are necessary. Changing a constitution is, as the late constitutional expert Senator Eugene Forsey put it in a Senate debate in 1976, very serious business: "It is not like getting a new hair-do, or growing a beard, or buying new furniture or new clothes, or putting in a new bathroom. It is more like marriage — in the words of the Anglican Prayer Book — 'not by any to be enterprised, nor taken in hand unadvisedly, lightly or wantonly... but reverently, discretely, advisedly, soberly, and in the fear of God.' What we are dealing with in constitutional change is not paper or things. It is human lives."

For decades that is precisely how constitutional change took place in Canada — each of the first seventeen amendments was made as a small and considered step. Old Age Pensions and Unemployment Insurance, for example, were each transferred by this process from the provincial to the federal level of authority. This incremental approach was successful in changing the Constitution while maintaining national unity. The Constitution was amended when it needed to be — not when politicians saw openings to bargain for advantages for themselves, their regions or their ethnic groups.

Then, in 1982, a "package deal" of patriation, constitutional amendment formula and *Charter of Rights and Freedoms* was introduced by Pierre Elliot Trudeau in a patriation story which is too long and too well-known to be repeated in detail here. Essentially, the Canadian government proceeded with amendments even though Quebec Premier René Lévesque would not sign the agreement.

The idea of constitutional "packages" caught on. Brian Mulroney, improving on a bad thing, constructed an even bigger and more controversial 1990 bundle, known as the Meech Lake accord. It had something for everybody. It not only gave Quebec its basic demands but it also offered the West a side deal of Senate reform which Mr. Mulroney agreed to adhere to as long as he was Prime Minister. Cartoons at the time showed a delighted Premier Robert Bourassa saying, in effect, "I went into the meeting asking for five things I wanted and I got seven!"

The process of negotiation and the content of the deal brought the country to the brink of disaster. The deal, which required the approval of Parliament and all ten provinces, fell apart when Manitoba and Newfoundland failed to ratify it. Instead of going back to basics with a smaller and more understandable package, the Mulroney administration allowed the deal to grow even more unmanageable. More and more interests — based on provincial, ethnic and special pressure groups — manoeuvered to advance their positions as part of one grandiose constitutional reform plan.

Now that an all-encompassing final package has been produced for Canada's approval it is time to get back to basics. Underlying the issue of constitutional reform is the very federal system itself which was the heart of the constitutional arrangement in 1867.

FEDERALISM: SOLUTION OR PROBLEM?

Canadians have a federalism fixation. They are the only people in the world who buy books on federalism at airport shops and actually read them. Their preoccupation is reflected in the classic story of students from four countries who were asked to write essays on different aspects of elephants. The American boldly entitled his treatise "Elephants and the Presidency"; the British student called hers "Elephants and the Monarchy"; while the French student preferred "Elephants and Sex." The Canadian, quite naturally, opted for "Elephants: A Federal or Provincial Responsibility?"

The federal fixation began with the constitutional system itself in 1867, when the British Parliament, at the request of the three colonies concerned, passed into law the *British North America Act*, formally establishing a semi-autonomous country on the northern border of the United States. New Brunswick, Nova Scotia, and the hitherto united lands of Ontario and Quebec came together to form a new country. In the years to come, six more provinces and two territories were formed, or joined, what became the second-largest independent country in the world.

The founding fathers established a federal form of government in order to accommodate regional, ethnic, language and other differences in a pluralistic state. Only a system of government which would allow each of the former (now provincial) governments some autonomy was considered acceptable. Moreover, the Fathers of Confederation believed that by giving the new provinces of Ontario and Quebec their own provincial governments and then re-uniting them as part of a larger unit, the former French colony would be able to peacefully co-exist within a larger union.

As we shall see, federalism turned out to be an even wiser decision than the founding fathers had anticipated. It proved to be the natural choice for Canada with its vast land mass, regional economies, language and cultural differences. Before Canadians lay the blame for their unity problems on the federal bargain and risk making matters worse by radical reconstruction of the political system, they should diagnose the country's problems very carefully and take another look at its beginnings.

Canadian Federalism: Origin and Evolution

When the Fathers of Confederation drew up the Constitution, they borrowed from the models of both Britain and the United States. They accepted the British parliamentary/cabinet system of government, and opted against what they viewed as the ramshackle congressional/presidential system of the United States. But they adopted some aspects of American-style federalism. The new Constitution gave power over important national interests to the federal government and those over "local" interests to the provinces.

Sir John A. Macdonald, Canada's first Prime Minister, advocated a strong central government with weak provincial governments which he thought should be assigned only "local" powers. Macdonald was a great admirer of American leaders, especially Madison. He called the American Constitution "one of the most skilful works that human intelligence ever created." Sir John's copy of Madison's draft constitution for the US is marked with the Canadian leader's own pencilled notations in favour of a strong central government.

Led by Macdonald, the original drafters of the *BNA Act* paid particular attention to the division of authority between federal and provincial governments. They granted the federal government all the powers considered important in the mid-19th century. These included defence, banking, taxation, and trade regulation as well as all other powers not specifically granted to the provinces and which did not involve religious, linguistic or cultural interests. The provinces, on the other hand, were given powers over what, at that time, were considered relatively minor matters, such as education, property and civil rights.

The United States had given the residual powers — the general but unnamed jurisdictions — to the individual states rather than to Washington. The Fathers of Confederation believed that this would weaken the central government too much, so these matters of "peace, order and good government" were retained federally. Over the years, US Supreme Court decisions and the federal government's vast finances have strengthened Washington at the expense of the states. The pattern has not been so clear in Canada.

In this country, judicial decisions in the early years altered the initial direction of authority. The Judicial Committee of the British Privy Council (Canada's superior court until 1947) simply expanded the meaning of some provincial jurisdictions, rather than accepting the residual clause of "peace, order, and good government." The shifting of power has not always gone in the same direction however. When new topics not mentioned in the *BNA Act* were introduced, such as aeronautics and uranium, the Supreme Court awarded jurisdiction to the federal government. On the other hand, the specific areas of control granted to the provinces in the *BNA Act* have also become more important. Medical care, social welfare and education are but a few examples of fields under provincial authority which have grown extensively.

Although they copied the American federal system, there were three other main features that the Canadian leaders omitted: an amendment formula, a bill of rights, and an elected Senate. In the early years, the lack of an amendment procedure was not felt, as Canada remained a member of the British Empire and was not completely independent in many respects. When Canadians wanted a constitutional amendment passed, they simply went to Britain to have it formally made into law. However, after full independence came with the 1939 *Statute of Westminster*, the lack of a constitutionalized amendment formula became an embarrassment.

In 1982, the Canadian government attempted to rectify some of these constitutional omissions. Prime Minister Pierre Elliot Trudeau, the federal parliament and nine provinces asked Britain to pass one final amendment — the *Canada Act*. When the Constitution was patriated, a Charter of Rights and five amendment formulae for making future changes came with it, giving the country two of the three missing constitutional provisions. However, there was no agreement about how Senators should be selected.

Wrangling over federal-provincial responsibilities and their associated financial arrangements began almost immediately after Confederation, but since 1982, the difficulties have plagued Canadian governments. Some underlying problems of federalism have never been resolved, especially those concerning Quebec, native peoples and the Senate.

Why Federalism?

Canadians are forever dissatisfied with and debating about how to change their brand of constitutional federalism. Was federalism the best possible choice? What are its comparative advantages and disadvantages?

There is much disagreement about the answers to these questions. Canadians tend to believe that federalism was established essentially to achieve the benefits of unification without loss of separate identities for the local units. Elsewhere, more grandiose arguments have been given to support federalism. Some say that federalism is synonymous with liberty, or that it protects minority rights. Still others believe that many of the so-called altruistic objectives attributed to federalism are inaccurate and misleading. They suggest that federalism is simply the result of regional political bargains and may be good, bad or indifferent, depending on the circumstances.

While the various sub-units in society hope to achieve gains from a federal union, they must also accept certain drawbacks. In order to realize their objectives, they have to give up some privileges and powers to a central government. Before doing this, they generally seek guarantees and safeguards so that they may maintain at least a degree of independent authority. Such guarantees are normally in the form of a written constitution, clearly dividing political authority and legal jurisdictions and spelling out limitations and restrictions.

One fundamental decision all federal regimes must make is how much power and authority to award to their regional governments. The degree of centralization can vary greatly from highly centralized to highly decentralized. Most of the world's 185 states are unitary in structure, that is, they have no state, provincial or regional governments which share final authority with the central institutions. Today, fewer than one-eighth of all states claim to be federal. In other words, the vast majority of states are more centralized than the twenty which are federal. And Canada is arguably one of the most decentralized federations of all.

There is a point beyond which it is dangerous to decentralize further. No one can say exactly where that point lies, but clearly Canada is coming close to it. When Canadians are tempted to take the easy way out in constitutional reform and opt for even more decentralization, they should think of the old saying: be careful what you ask for — you may get it.

When Do Federal States Fall Apart?

Federal constitutional arrangments are designed to accommodate regional, ethnic or other differences in a pluralistic state. When there is a high degree of homogeneity in a country, a unitary, majoritarian model of democracy will generally work well. As societal pluralism increases, other forms of democracy may be required. When societal cleavages are great, only a federal form of authority will suffice to keep a state united.

Whether highly divided federal regimes can hold together over time depends on the precise constitutional arrangements and also on the ability of political leaders to minimize societal differences. Leaders have to appreciate the dangers of fragmentation and transcend the hostilities inherent in divided societies. Citizens, on the other hand, must be prepared to accord legitimacy to their leaders both at the national and provincial levels. Whether this can be accomplished in any given situation is conditioned by how leaders have handled past conflicts, as well as by the current motivations of the public and the elite.

Studies of comparative federalism indicate that extremely ethnically-diverse states which exhibit low support for the regime and a lack of competent leadership, are apt to implode. Does Canada now have these conditions?

In a celebrated work on comparative federalism, Ronald Watts, recently an advisor to Prime Minister Mulroney, concluded that, historically, federal regimes have failed for four reasons:
1. Regional divergence of demands,
2. Weak communications,
3. A diminution of the original impetus for federal union, and
4. External influences.

This summary, although useful as a starting point, has one major flaw; all four factors are present in every federation to some degree, and they have been present in Canada since before 1867. Regional stresses and strains are to be expected in every federation, and therefore cannot adequately explain why some federations fail and others do not. Clearly, some federal systems do disintegrate. The Soviet Union and Yugoslavia are dramatic recent examples of federal systems which failed in their attempts to unite people of different languages, cultures and religious beliefs.

Watts' four factors, in themselves, will not cause Canada's collapse. They may make government difficult, but not impossible. However, lack of trust in institutions and politicians, incompetent leadership, and a multi-party system may constitute a trigger for the collapse of a federation when these factors listed by Watts become extreme. Keep these four factors in mind when we examine the origin of public cynicism, at the end of this chapter, and the depth of it in Canada at the end of the next chapter. It is the congruence of these four factors combined with high public cynicism and weak leadership that is particularly dangerous in Canada today.

When a federal system does break up, the separation is rarely cordial. Since the Second World War, no solidly based, sovereign and democratic federal state has experienced a peaceful secession. One has to go back to the turn of the century, when Norway divided from Sweden, to find a somewhat comparable, peaceful analogy. History is clear. War is the usual means by which states have divided. And break-ups of federal states have been followed by bitterness, division and civil unrest. We should expect this to be the case if Quebec separates from Canada.

The Imaginary Options

In *Alice in Wonderland*, Alice was told that if you don't know where you want to go, any road will take you there. Unlike many politicians today, the Fathers of Confederation did know where they wanted Canada to go, and they chose the best route available. Their goal was a strong, federal country in which all Canadians could maximize their opportunities. There were only a very few roads from which to choose; the models of governing were, and still are, limited.

Of course, like choosing a car, there are always fancy accessories that can be added, but when it comes to the basic, stripped-down models there are only a few possibilities. In this case, the basic choice was, and still is, a unitary, a confederal or a federal system of government. Sovereignty-association, the cherished option favoured by René Lévesque and many separatists today, is merely independence with bells and whistles.

Keith Spicer, as head of the 1991 Citizen's Forum on Canada's Future, declared himself "totally indifferent if we have a federal, confederal or sovereignty-association type of regime." Since these are terms for dramatically different constitutional arrangements, which are not interchangeable without great costs, he seemed to be saying it doesn't matter which form Canada chooses.

But it does matter.

Unitary government was never a serious option for Canada. The country is simply too vast and diverse to be governed by one powerful, central political authority. The choice was between federation or confederation. In a confederation, member states delegate limited authority to a central government. This choice was unpopular with the Fathers of Confederation. They had observed with concern just how difficult it was for the United States to manage a confederacy. After breaking from Britain, the thirteen colonies of the United States had initially formed a loose, quarrelsome confederacy. George Washington had warned then that "thirteen Sovereignties pulling against each other, and all tugging at the federal head [would] soon bring ruin on the whole." The country was on the verge of disintegration when it was transformed into a strong, federal union.

When the first Canadian colonies were linked together in 1867, they were mistakenly called a confederation. The arrangement was never confederal, but federal. The existing colonies were united under a central government, while retaining only limited areas of jurisdiction for themselves as provinces.

However, the idea of confederacy retains a superficial attraction which tantalyzes many nationalists and separatists in particular. In the basic confederal model, units band together loosely without giving up their sovereignty or independence. At first glance it seems to be a way to have independence while maintaining all the privileges afforded by belonging to a bigger unit — like having a well-stocked winecellar and drinking it all, too.

Unfortunately, politics does not work that way. Confederacies are notoriously fractious and unstable because they lack centralized leadership and control. They rarely survive. Regions and provinces prove selfish and pull in different directions. They try to maximize their own benefits and don't worry much about the costs for their partners or for the unit as a whole.

A better and more modern comparison with Canada is the European Community. In fact, it is often taken as an example of what

Quebec elites want. Many, including Quebec Premier Robert Bourassa, and his separatist opponent Jacques Parizeau, have argued that Canada should emulate it.

Bourassa believes the evolution of the European Community illustrates that political unity must follow economic unity. Parizeau believes the EC shows how well sovereign states can do by retaining their independence while keeping an economic link. Bourassa is right. Those who argue that the European Community is headed to a weak confederate form of government simply do not understand what is going on in Europe.

The European Community may fairly be called a confederation now, but it is already losing this status. It is moving at full speed to become a quasi-federal union, so that as a combined force it can achieve an economic competitiveness that the member countries cannot reach individually. The twelve member states are giving up a degree of sovereignty and building a political union with responsible institutions and democratic legitimacy.

It is no longer valid to write about the European Community as only a "common market." Europe is building a political union; it already has a measure of "pooled sovereignty," with many common institutions and policies. The Community's objective, as stated in the *Single European Act,* which becomes valid by the end of 1992, is not a confederacy, but a full-blown political union. The Maastrict treaty, although temporarily thrown off course, will provide a common currency, central European bank and common foreign and possibly even defense policies by the end of the century. The treaty also calls for greater powers for Parliament and more qualified voting (i.e., not unanimous) for decisions by the European Council. When Maastrict, or its successor treaty, is ratified, Europe will have taken a large step toward political integration.

What Europeans want to achieve, Canada already possesses. If Canada moves to a highly decentralized union, Canada and Europe will be like two speeding trains passing in opposite directions. While

Europeans are achieving greater unity, Canada will be being torn apart by centrifugal forces.

As the basis of their new federal arrangement, Europeans are clarifying jurisdictions by determining which level of government can deliver services most economically. This is what Canada ought to be doing: making rational, cost-effective decisions about which level of government should have which jurisdictions, not throwing out federalism and starting again.

It should now be obvious that Canada cannot have a unitary system. And it should also be obvious that a highly decentralizing strategy, such as sovereignty-association, would be a recipe for disaster — leading to either the break-up of the country or to eventual absorption into the United States. Today, in a highly competitive world which is moving more and more toward huge, powerful economic blocs, further decentralization would mean fragmenting our assets — and weakening the country.

Where Does Canada Go Now?

The choice of federalism was the best option for the country in 1867. It remains the best option today. Canada has existed peacefully and prosperously for 125 years. This is not to say that the impact of divisions over the federal Constitution has not been onerous, particularly economically.

The primary difficulty is that Quebec, aboriginal and regional interests demand decentralization of the federal government, while a strong central authority is required to direct a strong, competitive economy. It may be impossible to satisfy both these requirements at the same time. Certainly it cannot be done without competent leadership, backed up by public confidence in federal institutions.

In the 1990s, pressures for decentralization or devolution of powers from the central government seem insatiable. Yet of the few federal states in existence, Canada is arguably already the first or second most decentralized. Its constitutional, financial and cultural bases give it a relatively weak central government compared to other countries. With further decentralization Canada risks becoming a loose, quarrelsome confederation of almost-independent states.

Before they agree to make *any* changes in the Constitution political leaders should answer the following important question: How far can Canadians accommodate regional, provincial, linguistic and ethnic interests without decentralizing Canada to the point where it is too weak to compete in a global economy, and bereft of influence in international relations? Unless this question is answered, federal-provincial efforts to change the Constitution will merely be building on a termite-ridden foundation.

Provincial leaders have a personal, selfish stake in augmenting provincial power at the expense of the federal government. The strongest demands for decentralization come from the leaders of Quebec. They should be resisted. In truth, the average Quebecker really does not care much about decentralizing the country by transferring massive powers to the provinces. Quebec francophones feel closer to their provincial government than to the federal government. They regard provincial politicians as part of their extended family. But it does not necessarily follow that they want a massive devolution of powers to the provincial level, just assured cultural survival.

When an American state is dissatisfied with its lot because of some new law or regulation from Washington it protests vociferously. In Canada, dissatisfied provinces often threaten to take their marbles and go home — to separate from the country. That does not mean that they actually would. Separatist and regionalist movements have arisen with cyclical regularity both in Quebec and in the West. Their grievances need to be addressed, but solutions must be found within the realm of what is best for Canada as a whole — and that is federalism.

Only a few generalizations can be offered in this chapter about the details of federal arrangements. Jurisdictions such as the economy, trade and foreign policy clearly belong to the largest unit of government because of the complex and competitive nature of the international system. Fragmenting authority in these areas would reduce the ability of Canada to compete and prosper. This argument is compounded by the fact that Canada is experiencing economic difficulties because of the changing nature of the world economy and the adverse effects of the free trade deal with the United States.

Canadians must realize that the country is experiencing a fiscal crisis and far too high levels of unemployment already. Our future prosperity requires that we recognize the benefits of economic and monetary union and the consequent necessity of at least the current level of political integration. Without a strong federal government, power would eventually flow to another government such as the United States or to a supra-national institution.

Jurisdictions relating to culture and language, on the other hand, could be relegated to the lower, provincial units of government. This is broadly what the Fathers of Confederation — both English and French — wisely decided in 1867. Among the multitude of other opportunities, we could readjust federal-provincial powers in areas such as job training and immigration without major disruption to the economic and political system.

In the present situation, the Prime Minister and lesser politicians are attempting to undertake comprehensive reform of the Constitution under extremely negative conditions. Weak federal leadership has exacerbated strong demands from Quebec, native peoples and the West for extreme decentralization. These events have given rise to low support for federal politicians and lack of confidence in government institutions. It is a dangerous time for Canada.

The key figure in determining what the changes will be and how and when they will be implemented is the Prime Minister. Whoever occupies that office deserves the credit and the blame for much of what happens to Canada. The office has acquired very significant powers at the expense of Parliament, and this makes it particularly risky for the country to be subjected to weak leadership at this time.

PRIME MINISTERIAL POWER: IS IT TOO GREAT?

After the form of government itself, the second problem in Canada's current political climate is the weight of Prime Ministerial power, which continues to grow at the expense of Parliament, making federal institutions top-heavy and incapacitated.

Just what powers does the Prime Minister really have? What are the constraints? What are the opportunities, responsibilities and resources against which we can measure the top leader? In short, what sort of job is the Prime Minister supposed to be doing for Canada?

Much of the debate about the Constitution in Canada today is really about "political power" not about "jurisdictional powers." Power is the ephemeral, intangible Holy Grail of those in political life. It hovers somewhere in the air about the Prime Minister, the central figure in Canadian politics. What is this magic stuff that has eluded all but eighteen Canadians in the history of the country?

Power

Journalists constantly refer to power as a substance — something tangible that people can hold or grasp, but it is obviously not that simple. It could, for example, be the result of social relationships rather than something physical that can be possessed like gold. In many ways, governmental power is layered, like an onion. One can peel away successive layers of onion in search of its essence at the centre. But when all the layers are gone there is nothing left. Only the relationship between the layers has created the onion. And so it is with governmental power.

Power, both influence and coercion, has been part of the vocabulary of politics since the time of Machiavelli in the fifteenth century. Yet power remains enigmatic both to define and to acquire. Elusive as it is, most people would agree that power consists of the ability to make others do what one specifically wants — something that they would not otherwise do. It implies both personal influence and the ability to coerce others by threatening, or merely implying, the possible use of sanctions.

There can be no doubt that a great degree of this substance called power clings to the office of the Prime Minister. Governments are often referred to by the name of the person who holds the office — the Trudeau government, or the Mulroney government, for example. However, the eighteen individuals who have occupied that office have not all been able to grasp and use power to the same degree.

There are two important aspects of power which we must keep in mind. Firstly, a Prime Minister's power is not a "constant," it is relative both to other parts of the political system and to other Prime Ministers. One Prime Minister, perhaps because of personality or other intangible factors, is more or less powerful than another, or than Cabinet, or, say, than provincial premiers. Secondly, a Prime Minister's power is limited in two major ways: by formal institutional arrangements and by tradition. There are laws and regulations which govern the leader's behaviour and there are unwritten bounds which cannot be overstepped.

The PM's Levers of Power

The power which accrues to the office of Prime Minister may be viewed as a control panel with several different levers. The mere knowledge that the Prime Minister has the capacity to use these levers affords a great deal of power to the occupant of that position. He or she has already been elected to Parliament, chosen as national leader of the party at a leadership convention, and has led his or her party to victory at the polls. This direct link with the people provides enormous legitimacy, a kind of blank cheque to go ahead and pull the levers of power with the country's blessing. As leader of the party and holder of this mandate, the Prime Minister can command obedience and support from Cabinet ministers and backbenchers alike.

Some of these sources of power — the electoral success, the public prestige, the high reputation — are only temporary, and diminish when things begin to go wrong. When this happens, however, some of the purely legal aspects of power remain as lasting sources of influence.

Cabinet

Within the government party, a great deal of the leader's power centres on the ability to choose and chair the political elite of the country — the federal cabinet. The choice is not wide open, however. All Prime Ministers since confederation have encountered restrictions in choosing their teams. In fact, Sir John A. Macdonald once described his occupation as "cabinet-maker" to show how much energy had to go into the selection of personnel.

There is a familiar ritual to cabinet-making. It often precedes a new session of Parliament. Each time, regardless of which party is in power, there is public criticism of the Prime Minister and his ability to choose wise and appropriate ministers. The charge is invariably accompanied by the notion that major cabinet changes are necessary, but that only a few cosmetic adjustments will be made.

There is some justification for this widespread public skepticism. As long as one party holds power the most senior faces remain basically the same, only the titles change. Criteria such as intelligence and expertise may not be primary considerations. In fact, one sometimes wonders if they are even on the list. The story of an MP who was told he would not be selected for the Cabinet because he was not talented enough illustrates the point. The unfortunate hopeful pleaded that he was not asking to be made a senior public servant, only a cabinet minister.

The Prime Minister's hands are tied to a certain extent in terms of balancing personal characteristics and merit with the need to select a cabinet which is representative of the region, province, city, occupation and gender of Canadians. The major traditional constraint is regionalism. Prime Ministers adhere rigidly to the convention that there must be at least one minister from each province. (When he had no MPs west of Manitoba, Trudeau assigned four Senators from that region.) Such constraints prevent dramatic shifts in cabinet personnel. To remain with tradition, for example, ministers from each province in the west and east of the country often cannot be dropped, and this leaves only Ontario and Quebec in which the Prime Minister can manoeuvre. Meanwhile, eager, young — and often not so young — MPs wait in droves to replace cabinet ministers who might be less than outstanding in their jobs, or offend the Prime Minister.

This cabinet-maker's straitjacket was conceived and put into place while Canada was a very different country than it is today. In this era when specialization is so important, Prime Ministers should consider disregarding these traditional restrictions and adopting a wider selection for Cabinet material.

Patronage

Another valuable lever is the control of patronage appointments. The most important appointments, of course, are of the Cabinet members, but there is a host of other "carrots" in the Prime Minister's patronage bag: promotion to parliamentary secretary or committee chairman; appointment of Judges and Senators (at least for now!); and numerous positions in the public service, public corporations and Crown agencies, and, of course, party appointments. When the patronage-starved Tories came to power in 1984 they quickly surveyed the situation and discovered about 3300 Liberal appointees on federal boards, commissions and Crown corporations — some appointed "at pleasure" (their position could be revoked at any time) and others for fixed periods.

Perhaps the general public was made most aware of this source of Prime Ministerial power when Trudeau left massive patronage appointments for his successor, John Turner, to implement in 1984. Although everyone in politics knew this was normal practice, the Conservatives (aided by the media) cried foul and appeared to be scandalized. In this case, far from being a source of power for John Turner, patronage led to his undoing.

In arguably the most memorable moment of the leaders' television debates on July 24, 1984, Prime Minister Turner maintained that he had no option but to appoint a large number of nominees as requested by outgoing Prime Minister Trudeau. In high drama, Mulroney pointed an accusing finger and viciously attacked: "You had an option, Sir. You could have said, I'm not going to do it. This is wrong for Canada, and I'm not going to ask Canadians to pay the price. You had an option, Sir, to say no, and you chose to say yes to the old attitudes and the old stories of the Liberal party. That, Sir, if I may say respectfully, that is not good enough for Canadians."

This scene, replayed many times during the 1984 election, had a major effect on Mulroney and his advisors. Because of this success, they believed that they should do something about parliamentary reform.

Notwithstanding his dramatic pose, during the Tory leadership campaign, Brian Mulroney had earlier exclaimed, "There will be jobs for Liberals and NDP's too — after I have been Prime Minister for fifteen years and I can't find a living, breathing Tory in the country." Then, during the heat of the election itself he was overheard to say, "There's no whore like an old whore. If I had been in Bryce's [Mackasey] position I'd have been right in there with my nose in the public trough like the rest of them." Nevertheless, he called the Liberal appointments of John Turner "vulgar, shameful, outrageous."

As his double standard became clear, Mulroney told a highly-placed Tory, "You've got to get me off the hook on this one."

In normal practice, however, it is considered not nice, but normal, that a Prime Minister use these patronage selections to make his or her influence felt throughout the governmental structure. To quote Brian Mulroney again, "you dance with the lady what brung you." Legally, the appointments are recommendations of appointment, which are forwarded to the Governor General for approval. But a Prime Minister's appointees are never rejected — in fact, the Prime Minister also selects the Governor General.

The Party and the Next Election

Another important lever comes from being party leader in a system which features disciplined parties. The government relies on cohesion among its backbenchers to keep it in office and get its legislation through the House. Party leaders, especially Prime Ministers, have a number of sanctions at their disposal to strongly encourage backbenchers to toe the party line, culminating with the threat of expulsion from the party. Winning a seat without official party backing is highly improbable.

The lever of party discipline leads directly to the next source of authority. Sizeable revolts can always be met by the Prime Minister with a threat of dissolution of Parliament. The fear of being among those turfed out of Parliament in the normally high turnover of seats at every general election generally seems to quell dissent, especially among backbenchers who represent marginal constituencies.

Constraints on Prime Ministerial Power

Besides the restictive customs about cabinet-making, political institutions impose constraints on the Prime Minister in other ways. They limit the leader's ability to implement his or her ideas or vision for the country.

Perhaps the most severe restriction occurs in the minority government situation, when the electorate has not awarded the government party enough MPs to out-vote the combined opposition. This has occurred in about half the elections since the Second World War. In such circumstances, the PM's job is difficult, and the ability to negotiate is vital in terms of getting legislation passed.

There are other practical limitations on the Prime Minister besides the size of the government majority. Deadlines, routine business and parliamentary procedure all present restrictions. And, of course, there are limitations on the Prime Minister from outside Parliament. The Canadian federal system of government is a labyrinth of walls and hurdles for a federal leader to work within or try to scale.

Canadians who vote and sit in constant judgment on their elected Prime Minister also limit the framework within which he or she can operate. As leader-in-chief, the PM is assured of national attention, but as many have discovered to their chagrin, this can be a curse as well as a blessing. To stay on top of the greasy pole the PM must persuade voters of his or her worth, skilfully arranging the legislative timetable to distract them from harsh economic realities that might cause a fall from those lofty heights at election time.

Rules limit Prime Ministerial action, and lack of constraints may actually enhance those limitations. There are two particular areas where a lack of adequate rules concerning the Prime Minister is a handicap to the Canadian public. One is the lack of rules governing leadership succession in an emergency, and the other is the unlimited tenure of Prime Ministers.

What would happen in Canada if the Prime Minister died or resigned from office tomorrow? There is no precedent. Since 1919, party leaders have been chosen by conventions, a system which works well under normal circumstances, but is slow and unwieldy in an emergency. In case of a sudden leadership vacuum it has generally been assumed that the parliamentary caucus would choose an interim

Prime Minister until a convention could be held. But what if there were no clearly favoured candidate, or a deadlock within the parliamentary party? In that case, the Governor General might well have to consult senior party members and use the royal prerogative to name someone, as was done on a regular basis in the 19th century.

The latter situation would allow the Governor General unwarranted authority in a modern democracy. And temporary appointments while waiting for a convention could cause months of economic and political uncertainty. Lester Pearson wanted to call a leadership convention as soon as possible after he decided to retire in the early 1960s, but Keith Davey informed him that the soonest it could be arranged would be four months. Pearson complained that such a delay was "crazy," and he was right.

The rules of succession in the event that a Prime Minister abruptly leaves office are inadequate. The precedents are too vague and *ad hoc* to be relied on.

A second problem is that there is no limit to the number of terms a Prime Minister can serve, so that political leaders may remain in office an inordinately long time — or what seems like "forever" to political opponents, other leadership hopefuls, and a weary public. Since the Constitution provides no restrictions on the number of terms a Prime Minister may remain in office, they are all perpetually re-eligible. They seldom leave office on their own initiative or are kicked out by their colleagues. Most have had to be booted out by the electorate at a general election before they stood down. With only eighteen Prime Ministers in 125 years, Canada's top leaders have had one of the highest durability records in the democratic world.

Prime Ministerial Government?

Behind the constitutional myths and dictums about how Canada ought to be governed, there is a harsh reality. The federal Parliament and also the provincial legislatures are dominated by their respective executives. The power of legislatures is weak throughout the western world, but nowhere more so than in Canada. Parliament has not kept up with other institutions in society in terms of organizational characteristics, influence or resources. The Prime Minister controls cabinet, caucus and indeed Parliament, because of an interlocked set of factors which involves the relations among the legislature, parties and the media. Prime Ministerial power is a bit like high blood pressure. It doesn't hurt, and you can't see it, but it can cause extensive damage.

The fact that the political system is dominated by the executive at the expense of Parliament is not new, and not even undesirable. But alarming changes have taken place in executive-legislative relations at the federal level over the past decade and a half. The legislative-executive balance has become too heavily weighted to the executive during the Mulroney era, so that the democratic responsiveness of the system is compromised. One effect of this is the current clamour to strengthen provincial power in Canadian politics.

The Canadian form of government was conceived to be "similar in principle to that of the United Kingdom," close to the British cabinet-ministerial model. In the early years of Confederation party cohesion was weak; being a Member of Parliament was not considered a full-time position, and the media was inconsequential. The House of Commons and Senate played important roles in the development of ideas and policies. Decisions were taken by individual ministers acting in collaboration with the Prime Minister, or, in important situations, by Cabinet as a whole.

However, changes in party organization soon affected the relationship between the executive and Parliament. Party discipline impeded the ability of backbenchers in the House of Commons to rebel against their leaders. And, the first election of the leader of the party by a party convention in 1919 further elevated the Prime Minister above his colleagues.

Today it is sometimes argued that Canadians have "presidentialized" the Prime Minister in that he can overstep his proper authority, and that this fact portends grave consequences for responsible government and the parliamentary system. The Prime Minister's ideas become cabinet policy, which becomes government policy, which in turn is foisted onto backbenchers, who have little choice but to vote in obedience to the party, and then onto the general public.

Within Cabinet the Prime Minister exercises extensive power without having to say much. A personal experience in a Trudeau Cabinet gave the following insight. Allan J. MacEachen made a persuasive case for reform of Canada's political institutions, and all of his colleagues around the table, in turn, supported his argument. But when Mr. Trudeau "summed up," as was his custom, he shrugged and said, "I don't know, Allan, let's discuss it next week." They returned to the topic a few days later. Without debate all of the ministers around the table, one after the other, said that on consideration they had changed their minds, and now disagreed with the proposal. The file was closed.

The argument of Prime Ministerial dominance is somewhat exaggerated. The Prime Minister must still obtain the agreement or aquiescence of cabinet members and caucus, and can not simply order them about. Ministers and members have some independent authority within caucus and usually in their regions. Moreover, in about half the parliaments since the Second World War, Prime Ministers have had to manoeuvre minority governments in which they did not control a majority of Members of Parliament. Contrary to myth, some Prime Ministers even have been kicked out of office — Meighen in 1926, Diefenbaker in 1963 and Clark in 1979.

Nevertheless, the march toward Prime Ministerial government has been relentless. By 1945, cabinet committees began to develop. Prime Ministers and their cabinet colleagues amassed new resources and personnel. Cabinets gradually doubled in size. By 1984 the cabinet had forty members, the largest number in Canadian history. Today it is thirty-nine. Large cabinets proved to be inefficient, so authority began to move elsewhere. The Cabinet performed more like a sounding board for the Prime Minister than a deliberating body. Prime Ministers had to establish small committees to direct their activities.

Throughout the Trudeau, Clark, Turner and Mulroney terms a sociological, inner group model developed in which the most important decisions were taken by a small group of ministers and senior advisers, along with the Prime Minister. Prime Minister Mulroney has gone beyond even an informal inner group. He has set up a powerful Priorities and Planning Committee which can act in the name of Cabinet, and he has created a small operations committee which controls access to it and thus can shape the choices and timing of decisions. A "communications" committee has been set up to provide "appropriate" information on all government activities.

Characteristically, Mr. Mulroney has also set up an "institutionalized" inner group model to handle economics. Three committees — Treasury Board, Priorities and Planning, and Expenditure Review —monopolize much of the influence. Only half of the ministers sit on these three committees and yet they are the only ones to control over-all budgetary allocations and revenue decisions. Thus, more than half the ministers have been reduced in importance — downgraded, as one disgruntled minister told us, to the status of "eunuchs."

Changes in cabinet structure, party discipline and the election of the leader at a party convention are not the only reasons for the development of independent Prime Ministerial authority. By the mid 1960s, a new development in Canadian politics significantly strengthened the hand of an already dominant Prime Minister and executive. An electronic age of politics replaced the earlier "patronage" and "brokerage" periods.

In this era of "electronic politics" there is a love-hate relationship between politicians and the media. Members of both the press and electronic media believe they exploit politicians. Politicians think they manipulate the media. The relationship is fickle, and a mélange of facts and opinions are relayed to the public concerning political circumstances, character, and moods. As the two sides manipulate each other, the public is left with considerable knowledge about personalities and transient issues but very little understanding of the real impact of policies and laws on citizens. This is an era of "value politics" in which the "values" expressed by the leader on television count more in elections than party identification or program commitment.

In this game of personalized, electronic politics, the leader has become electorally indispensable to the party and infinitely less at risk of attack by his colleagues than formerly. With three-quarters of the population receiving all their information about politics from television, the Prime Minister's dominant role is beyond question. His colleagues in Cabinet and caucus simply understand that the image conveyed about the Prime Minister is vital for their own election success. As with President L.B. Johnson, they may say privately, "he may be a corrupt SOB but he's our SOB."

It was Prime Minister Trudeau who greatly expanded the role of the central agencies around Cabinet. The importance of the political staff to the Prime Minister (Prime Minister's Office) and the closest public servants (Privy Council Office) were enhanced. The role of pollsters and communications specialists grew.

Under Mr. Mulroney this has been refined. Every cabinet memorandum requires a "communications plan" and public servants are required to assess the role interest groups will play in regard to the proposed policy. As it was so well said by the British television serial, "Yes, Minister," the ship of state is the only ship which leaks from the top. The preponderance of senior civil servant discussions preceeding Cabinet meetings concerns one subject — the enormous public relations operation that will need to be mounted with each government action in order to present the administration in the best possible light.

Professional public servants today are unable to overcome the trend to the powerful inner circle around the Prime Minister. Instead, they hone their chameleon-like abilities to evince enthusiasm and political sensitivity toward the policies of whatever leader is in power. No public servant, however senior, stands up to the Prime Minister or inner group to indicate that there may be a national interest, as opposed to a political interest, at stake in a government policy.

The Prime Minister is more than *primus inter paris* or "first among equals." He dominates the Canadian political scene as absolutely as any monarch did during the age of the divine right of kings. When he shrugs, sets his jaw or glowers, ministers, public servants and Parliament fall in line quickly or they are out of office. As one senior public servant said about Quebec Premier Maurice Duplessis, it is "not healthy to resist the orders" of the Prime Minister.

PARLIAMENT: IS IT TOO WEAK?

With the rise of powerful Prime Ministers, there has been a corresponding lament that the executive has grown too powerful at the expense of the legislature. No one believes that Parliament should be weak. Indeed, there seems to be almost unanimous agreement that it should be the dominant body in settling the philosophical and political differences which exist within the country.

At the same time, however, a general pessimism exists that nothing can be done to buttress the failing legislature. The legitimacy of the institutions is not questioned, but what is doubted is the ability of legislators to perfom their tasks in government policy-making and in surveillance of the executive. It is also clear that as long as legislators invite ridicule, whether deserved or not, they cannot play an effective part in the overall political process. Certainly, legislatures need more credibility and will gain it only when they are strengthened and brought in line with other institutions of the near-21st century.

Undoubtedly, legislatures are weak for many reasons. The basic structures of the legislature developed in a period when a different kind of society and government existed. In the 19th century when Parliament began, there were neither radios nor televisions, household work was not highly mechanized, the world was not circled by air routes, and communications satellites did not provide instant contact on a world-wide basis. The constant advance of complex technology has reduced the unique role which legislatures played a century ago. But there are also some particular political reasons behind the changing role of the Canadian legislature.

Reforming the Legislature

There have been many attempts in recent years to initiate reform which would redress the growing imbalance between legislature and executive. Unfortunately, the changes have ended up strengthening the executive instead. During Pierre Trudeau's Prime Ministership, procedural changes strengthened executive control over House business. Closure and time allocation, once considered dictatorial devices, became accepted as necessary government tools.

During the early years of Mr. Mulroney's term as Prime Minister, the so-called McGrath reforms were introduced. Some of the reforms were brilliant, while others missed the mark completely. Recommendations for the end of party discipline, for example, were romantic nonsense.

The most important of the recent parliamentary reforms concerned organization. They include the election of the Speaker by secret ballot, the development of an Internal Economy Committee without ministers, and improved private-members' bill procedures. Standing committees are now able to determine their own terms of reference and to demand that the government respond to their proposals. To some extent, Committee size, organization and support structures have also improved.

Less successful changes were also made in committees of the House of Commons. The division of the committees into two types — standing and legislation — has made it difficult to maintain the necessary surveillance of the executive. The temporary Legislation Committees, which die at the end of the discussion of each new bill, have added very little to the process. Taking the functions of handling bills away from the permanent Standing Committees has reduced their power to act as independent power centres in Parliament.

If there is to be parliamentary influence, the committees must be strengthened even more, not weakened. Strong legislatures tend to have strong committee systems. And committees are strong only when they are few in number, their membership is limited, their ability to investigate subjects is unhampered by government, and they have their own budgets and payrolls. Even after the McGrath reforms, the Canadian parliamentary committee system meets few of these conditions.

The worst reform has been that which many thought would increase parliamentary control over the executive. After the McGrath reforms, the House of Commons obtained the ability to scrutinize — i.e. study, but not veto — all order-in-council appointments made by the government. Even the McGrath report said this would throw Members of Parliament "into uncharted waters." But it is worse. The new power may yet prove the cynic's law of parliamentary reform — that the unintended consequences always outweigh the improvements achieved. The scrutiny rules will weaken the executive because bargaining with the House will have to take place not only on legislation and financial matters, but also on that of government personnel. All of this will not be evident until the next minority goverment — which may be soon.

In all, the legislative process has been substantially changed over the past 25 years. The system of executive -legislative relations works fairly well, but is increasingly controlled by the executive, which is more and more driven by a small Prime Ministerial inner group.

To a great degree, governing and democratic responsiveness are not compatible, but Parliament ought to play a role in both spheres. Those who believe that partisan "show biz" is all there is to governing will object to this contention. But it is important to maintain an appropriate balance between executive leadership and legislative influence. There is a need for a "working" legislature and a loosening of the executive grip on policy-making in Canada.

Party Discipline: Unpopular but Important

One of the silliest notions about Canadian politics these days is that party discipline should be disbanded in favour of "free" MPs. Even the House of Commons itself has joined the folly. The McGrath report called for significant "attitudinal" changes to allow MPs to stray from the party line. This declaration has had no discernible effect on MPs' behaviour, and it will not have any.

Such calls for attitude change will never be effective. Parties and MPs are kept together by more than "whips and carrots"; they are kept together by the desire to be re-elected at the next election, and by the same sociological pressures that exist in any group concerned with survival and success. In other words, they are held together by the members' own beliefs and attitudes about Canadian politics and the electoral habits of voters. MPs may tell their constituents that they vote a specific way because of party discipline, but the truth is, they do it because it is in their party's and their own self interest. There never was a "golden age" of Parliament when Canadian MPs were "loose fish." In the 19th century, there were times when the parties could not strictly control the behaviour of their MPs, but then they were reined in by financial and social ties.

The question should not be whether MPs are free to vote against their parties, but rather, in whose interests are they voting? Free voting would not mean that MPs were free of pressures to conform with another group's position. Is it better to have MPs' behaviour determined by widely based cohesive parties, or by narrower interest groups?

In our opinion, free votes and the consequential breakdown of party cohesion in Parliament is not desirable. Members could, however, exercise their individual responsibility in Ottawa more forcefully without harming either the party system or cabinet decision-making. The German system, where a clear distinction is made between "votes of confidence" which bring down governments and "votes on issues," should be explored, and reasonable amendments implemented in the Standing Orders of the House of Commons.

Should Constituents Control their MPS?

In their disillusionment with political leadership, Canadians from coast to coast are falling prey to the belief that their Members of Parliament should do precisely what they tell them to do or else resign. The Reform Party platform, which proposes such public participation devices as referendums and recall of MPs, has been perpetuating this nonsense. Irresponsibly, it wants the public at large, rather than Parliament, to decide issues. And it wants to be able to recall MPs — force them to resign and fight another election — when they do not vote as their constituents say they should.

These are not new ideas; the debate about the appropriate relations between the elected representative and his or her constituents has been going on for over two centuries. The contemporary Canadian debate is simply superficial and without an adequate intellectual foundation.

In our opinion, complete independence for the representative from the wishes of the constituent would not be democratic, in that government would not be responsive to its citizens. On the other hand, it is not possible for a member to represent his constituents perfectly on every issue. He or she has no way of determining what they want on every topic. Nor is it likely that all constituents will agree on any given issue. And, let us be honest about this, constituents usually do not know what they want. Nor do they often care about issues that do not affect their personal lives.

The only way out of this dilemma, it would apear, is to elect representatives wisely and then allow them to exercise their best judgment about what is needed as circumstances arise. If constituents have strong views, the representatives will listen, if they want to be re-elected.

At the same time, voters must remember that legislators have values and feelings of their own about what is right and wrong. Members of Parliament have to maintain good working relationships with their colleagues in the House of Commons in order to accomplish anything. They are not without obligations to people other than their constituents. Once elected, representatives deserve some leeway to balance the many forces which impinge on them. They are not puppets, but neither are they mavericks.

Prime Ministers and lesser politicians are in disfavour in Canada at the moment, but grabbing back the responsibilities of making parliamentary decisions and subjecting MPs to recall procedures would be cumbersome, expensive and unduly threatening to the democratic process. Referendums also have serious drawbacks as regular decision-making processes. Perhaps most seriously, they do not accommodate compromise because the propositions must be stated in black and white terms, and obtain yes or no answers. As such, they tend to be very corrosive and divisive.

Reforming the Senate

One of the ironies of legislative reform today is that while the significance of the lower, elected house is declining, reformers are concentrating on strengthening the upper house. There is a reason for this. From the beginning, the appointment process of the Senate has been flawed. Since Confederation the membership has been appointed by the Prime Minister of the day. This adversely affects the legitimacy and credibility of both the appointees and the institution.

Since 1975, the membership of the Senate has been fixed at 104, with 24 each from the 4 main regions — Ontario, Quebec, the West (6 from each of the 4 provinces) and the Maritimes (10 each from New Brunswick and Nova Scotia, 4 from Prince Edward Island), together with 6 from Newfoundland and 1 each from the Yukon and the Northwest Territories. These Senators were originally appointed for life, but since 1965 they have had to retire at 75. Since the average Senator dies before the age of 75, this introduction of compulsory retirement has not reformed the age distribution of the upper house. Most of its members are senior citizens who are appointed solely for patronage reasons.

Efforts to reform the Senate are far from new. For decades, the upper house has weathered public scorn as an expensive, high-class retirement home for political has-beens. It has been caught in a catch-22 situation, ridiculed if it did not act and condemned if it did. Like the weather, senate reform has been a staple subject of serious discussion and political jokes. Prime Minister Mackenzie King, for example, once promised to substitute live Grits for dead Tories in the Upper Chamber. John Diefenbaker commented later that according to that criterion, some of King's appointees were only half qualified.

In any case, pressure for senate reform is, as one astute observer remarked, something that comes periodically, like other forms of "epidemics and current fevers." The truth is, the Senate is younger and more active today than it ever has been.

Whatever Happened to Sober Second Thought?

The Canadian Senate was established as an institution of sober second thought for government legislation. For years it worked quietly away and did just that. Then gradually, and with little fanfare following the election of the Mulroney government in 1984, the Liberal-dominated Senate began sharpening its teeth and tackling government bills. It exercised powers that many assumed had atrophied. The Senate was on the way to becoming "effective."

The powers to make the Senate effective had been there all along, they had just fallen into disuse. The current Senate cannot initiate money bills, and can only delay constitutional amendments for 180 days. But what it can do is introduce any non-money bill and amend or defeat any bill. Exercising that power would make the Senate exceedingly effective, indeed powerful.

Before the Mulroney government came to power in 1984, the Senate had not publicly blocked a bill since 1939. It had threatened to do so in 1961 when it delayed passage of a bill to remove James Coyne, then Governor of the Bank of Canada. But Coyne resigned, and that issue was resolved before the Senate had to exercise its will any further. The Senate lapsed into its traditional role of silently scrutinizing, but not rejecting, government bills.

Then, with the election of the Conservative government in 1984, a whole new set of circumstances came into play. The predominantly Liberal Senate grated under some of the policies of the new government. And, under the leadership of Allan MacEachen, a veritable wizard on parliamentary procedure, it had the expertise it needed to make its voice heard.

Early in the Mulroney government it appeared to some that the Senate had finally succumbed to rampant senility. After years of rubber stamping House of Commons legislation, the upper chamber was obstreperously blocking the first major financial bill presented by the new Conservative government. By frustrating the will of the

Conservative representatives in the Commons, Liberal Senators invited a virtual plague of reform on the Upper House.

Senator MacEachen also began dropping the Senate practice of "pre-study," saying that as a legislative body it had the right to insist that bills go first to the Commons, then to the Senate for study. This signalled that the Liberal majority in the Senate would no longer automatically approve all legislation submitted to it. Nor would it necessarily allow the government to reject its recommendations without a challenge.

After that, such challenges became persistent. In early 1985, the Senate held up the government's borrowing bill until the main estimates were tabled in both Houses. In the next session the Senate slowed down or significantly amended several other bills from the Commons and did not pass a number of others.

Rather than dutifully passing the remaining legislation without proper scrutiny as they usually did, in the closing days of the last session the Senate chose to let several bills die. The best remembered of these bills was undoubtedly the Government's Free Trade bill. By stalling it, the Senate effectively set the date for the 1988 general election.

Not only was the government forced to accommodate Senate requests to amend significant legislation, but as well, in one highly unusual case which acknowledged Senator MacEachen's strength, the Tory government went out of its way to get Senate approval. Bill C-147 (concerning the Canadian Centre for Human Rights and Democratic Development) would have died on the order paper if Joe Clark's office had not approached Senator MacEachen. Magically, within hours, the revised bill was adopted by the Senate, whizzed through the House of Commons and given Royal Assent the evening before the election was called.

This pattern of Senate revival continued after the 1988 election. The Unemployment Insurance legislation was seriously delayed, but the GST was the major challenge. Because it was so unpopular, the tax was an ideal opportunity for the exercise of Senator MacEachen's talents. Mr. MacEachen held up the tax and gave Canadians an effective Senate. Prime Minister Mulroney took it away again by appointing enough Conservatives to break the Liberal majority in the Senate. He took advantage of a controversial, exotic clause in the Constitution which allowed him to appoint eight extra Senators, filling the august body to the maximum possible of 112 members. The Conservatives were thereby ensured a majority in the Senate.

Considerable political damage accrued to Mr. Mulroney and the Conservatives in a backlash following this new binge of patronage appointments. The image of Parliament was tarnished once again. The government got away with appointing the eight extra Senators, but only because there was not a strong constitutional case against it.

Canadians have wanted to reform the Senate for decades, but have been unable to decide how to do it. Options are expensive and divisive. The history of the Senate during the Mulroney governments illustrates that it can be an effective body already, and without upsetting the existing pattern of government. It would be better to abolish it completely rather than create an institution that would cause continual stalemates with the House of Commons. The most serious problem remains lack of legitimacy because of the appointments procedure.

THE ORIGINS OF PUBLIC CYNICISM

A few rotten apples can spoil the whole bushel. The same is true of political leaders and backbenchers; the key is to root out the bad ones and leave the good ones alone. On the whole they are honest, hard-working and highly motivated to serve the public. However, only Prime Ministers, Members of Parliament and Senators themselves can do the rooting out. There are several steps they could take. They could, for example, get rid of rules which give them special priviledges, so that the same laws and the same treatment apply to all Canadians.

In the fall of 1990 MPs anguished over whether to restrict RCMP investigations on Parliament Hill. On the one hand, they wanted to be able to do their work free from intimidation, and, in particular, without worrying about unwarranted RCMP investigations which might blacken their personal reputations. On the other hand, they realized that if they allowed themselves different treatment than other Canadians suspected of breaking the law, they would blacken their collective reputation.

Common sense prevailed eventually and a Commons committee decided that police would *not* have to consult with a Commons Committee before applying for search warrants, or obtaining bugging authorizations against an MP or Senator under suspicion of criminally misusing office budgets or staff. The police would have the opportunity for consultation, but the procedure would not be mandatory. Police investigations, therefore, would not be delayed, allowing suspects time to destroy evidence.

At the heart of this debate was the argument by MPs and Senators that they have special regulations, budgets, tax-free exemptions and staffing rules that the public and the police do not understand. Police investigations can ruin careers, but special rules for MPs open the door to misunderstanding. But there is a better way; by not having any special rules for MPs, there would be no reason for MPs to worry about unwarranted police investigations, because there would be no regulations that could be misunderstood. The same standards of conduct would apply to all Canadians.

In line with this philosophy, our Members should get rid of all special budgets and tax-free exemptions to which they are now entitled. This does not mean that MPs should take salary or expense allowance cuts. They should get the same amount of money in real terms as they do now, but they should also be required to *account* for their deductions exactly like the rest of us. In early 1992, MP René

Soltens tried to get support for a private member's bill to make the tax-free allowance part of the normal income of Members of Parliament. He got no support from his colleagues. The bill did not even come to a vote.

If this reform were enacted, MPs would have to be given a salary increase. That might be unpopular, but at least it would be honest and open. In the long run, Canadians would stop believing that MPs were getting away with questionable expenses by hiding them in tax-free non-accountable allowances.

MPs in 1992 are paid a basic salary of $64,400, plus a tax-free allowance of $21,300 (equivalent to $41,846 in taxable earnings). Total earnings can therefore be calculated at $106,246. And then there are the perks: a staff of 5 or 6; 64 free round-trip plane rides to and from their constituency, a number of trips for family members; suites of offices in Ottawa and in the constituency, furnished with modern office machines; and the *pièce de résistance*, a fully indexed, generous pension of which other Canadians can only dream. Jean Lapierre, a former Liberal MP who defected and joined the Bloc Québécois in order to promote the break-up of Canada, resigned in the summer of 1992 with a pension of $40,000 for the rest of his life. This could be calculated at roughly 4 million dollars of taxpayers' money. It does leave room for cynicism!

Given the tenuous nature of the job, the expense involved in getting it, the salaries of professionals and the type of candidates Canadians want to attract to the job, the salary of a Member of Parliament is too low. It should be pegged in the range of a top public servant — about $150,000 with no special perks or tax breaks. All allowances should be accounted for by the same rules as other public servants, and the pensions should be equivalent to those of other government employees. It is sheer folly to attract public frustration, cynicism and outrage through the non-accountable personal use of public money.

Canadians are justifiably cynical about politicians when they see their elected members feathering their own nests while other nests are bare. Every year, the Auditor General exposes horror stories about government waste and mismanagement. Scandals and corruption are still rare enough to be news, but commonplace enough that nobody is surprised. Conflict-of-interest rules are regularly found to be too lax. All of this is at great cost to the taxpayer and feeds public cynicism. Legislative costs for the House of Commons alone amounted to more than $229 million in 1991-92. It is ironic that so much attention today is focused on Senate reform, and not on the performance and accountability of Members of the House of Commons.

MPs, as a whole, do not deserve their bad image. The best way to change that image is for them to be paid competitively and openly. But they should be treated the same as their fellow citizens before the law, with no special rules or privileges to hide behind.

The confrontational, and sometimes raucous, nature of Question Period is also often cited as a cause of public cynicism with the parliamentary process. It is argued that since television was introduced the public hears and sees much more of what transpires in the House. While it is true that the sometimes juvenile behaviour which surfaces in the House does the MPs involved no credit, Question Period is a very significant opportunity to question government ministers and make them accountable for their actions.

In spite of recurring complaints about deteriorating parliamentary behaviour, it is doubtful if parliamentary decorum has declined. The House has been, and continues to be, a raucous place during Question Period. Every few months, it creates headlines with stories of bell-ringing, name-calling and other shenanigans. But, in reality, there is little spontaneous behaviour in Question Period. The Speaker calls members from lists presented to him by the whips of the parties and the whole charade is choreographed in party caucuses.

None of this type of parliamentary behaviour is new. As an example, take the final days of the 1879 session of the Canadian Parliament in the staid and decorous Victorian era. In one particularly eventful sitting which Prime Minister Mackenzie could not control (Macdonald did not notice; he was asleep, drunk, outside the House), the uproar exceeded all previous and later periods. The debate lasted 27 hours, and was punctuated by the members roaring, singing songs, blowing toy trumpets and throwing Blue books across the floor. Lady Dufferin showed up twice, only to be received with the House rising to sing "God Save the Queen" until she fled, embarrassed. A Quebec member led a makeshift band with his toy bagpipe, until the Speaker ruled that this behaviour, and throwing Blue books, was unparliamentary. The Sergeant-at-Arms was instructed to restore order, but he had hidden to enjoy the fun and was not to be found.

"The Enemy is Us"

There are a host of other flaws in the system that promote dyspeptic public opinion and cynicism with politicians. One of the most blatant is the typical government's five-year "Scrooge" policy. Readers have undoubtedly noticed how closely the life-cycle of the typical government parallels Dickens' *A Christmas Carol*. It is a well-written story, full of conflict and irony. The scenario always begins with an idyllic community under siege by a terrible tyrant. Just when everyone is thoroughly convinced that Scrooge will reduce the place to a shambles, catastrophe is averted and Scrooge is acclaimed hero by all. The government plays the Scrooge role like clockwork every five years. In the first post-election year it bombards the public with unpopular proposals and taxes. During the ensuing two years it slowly pries open the state coffers and distributes increasingly larger goodies — such as submarine or helicopter contracts. Then, at the end of the fourth year, it astonishes all but a few cynics with declarations of good will and proposals to deliver the most wonderous gifts which are, however, almost never unwrapped before the next election. This five-year Scrooge policy tarnishes the reputation of all politicians.

Such blatant efforts to manipulate the public have made Canadians totally cynical about the political process. In particular, they are critical of the mutual manipulation of the press and politicians and their flagrant disregard for the concerns and interests of the people they are supposed to be serving. Nowhere is this more evident than in the public's attitudes toward political leaders, and particularly the Prime Minister.

The public's lack of trust and respect for the flawed institutions of government and weak leadership have been growing over time. This lack of public confidence is the real worry. It could be the trigger for the collapse of Canada. If "Canada is a dream in the making," as Roch Carrier says, then many of us now feel rudely awakened. It's time for our political leaders to hear the alarm bells too.

4 Leaders And Followers

"This is no time for on the job training; a leader must be a leader."

> **— Federal Liberal campaign slogan for 1979 general election (Trudeau vs. Clark)**

Almost every Canadian has ideas and opinions about the political leadership of this country. Most are not flattering. In fact, when we began to write this book and mentioned to friends that it would be about leadership, the most revealing response was, "it must be a short book!" The second most revealing comment was, "Canadian leadership? What is that — an oxymoron?"

Political leadership is desperately needed today. Public cynicism about leadership and government is at a record high in Canadian modern history; Canadians distrust and even denigrate their political leaders as incompetent and unequal to the job. Yet faith in leadership and the democratic process is essential to a country's economic and social well-being.

Political institutions are unable to keep in check the divisive tendencies generated by the ethnic and regional cleavages that exist in Canada today. That they were able to in the past was due, to a large extent, to good leadership. The first seventeen Prime Ministers created a vibrant Canada: they maintained a strong central government; they insisted that the state should be able to interfere in the economy when necessary; and they assured that the federal government would provide a social security net for the least fortunate in society. In doing so they retained public confidence in political institutions. However, the eighteenth Prime Minister, Brian Mulroney, has brought a new and divisive dialogue to Canadian politics — one based on a neo-conservative outlook and an ideology of difference — which has contributed to the decline in confidence in politicians, parties, leaders and governmental institutions alike. He has led Canada into a nightmare of interminable constitutional debates and toward a fragmented party system which could bring about stalemate government and possibly the break-down of the federal system itself.

Prime Minister Brian Mulroney and lesser politicians have let Canada down. But all Canadians must share some of the blame. There is a great deal of truth in the saying that people get the leadership they deserve. Canadians have been too readily hypnotized and led by the media; they are attracted by superficial qualities and showbiz glitz at the expense of quiet competence and strength of character.

Political leadership is an extremely difficult task in Canada today. Parties are less cohesive, the country is more fragmented, public opinion is angry and fickle, and special interests are more vocal and powerful than in earlier times. The media, especially television, is more significant in the political process than ever before. It could be a vital aid to the democratic process, but instead it is too often a hindrance, reducing ideas and personalities to meaningless phrases and caricatures.

EVALUATING LEADERS

Judging political leaders is fraught with pitfalls, though Canadians do it all the time. They have opinions about whether the current Prime Minister has a neo-conservative agenda or is merely reacting to events; they have kind things to say about some provincial premiers while they cannot even remember the names of others. Opinions are formulated with the assistance of various media which recall and repeat the successes and failures of politicians, surreptitiously molding public opinion while selectively refreshing memories.

It is often taken for granted that individuals who hold lofty political positions are leaders. Prime Ministers are called leaders. Premiers of provinces are called leaders. Heads of political parties are called leaders. In fact, Canadian political parties are unique in having "Leaders" with a capital "L." But leadership and office-holding are not necessarily the same thing. Those in public office do not exercise personal power and influence to the same degree. Some are merely pulled hither and thither by different interests. They do not lead.

Judgment about a leader, therefore, should be based on the personal traits an individual brings to the office as well as situational factors. Winnowing out the impact of a leader's qualities from larger phenomena such as history, culture and social and economic trends is exceedingly difficult, and it may never be possible to untangle completely the web of historical causation. For this reason many experts tend to view leadership as a relationship between leaders and followers; the major test becomes the leader's ability to mobilize followers and bring about viable change.

Canadians need some fair criteria by which to judge their leaders. Serious analysis of political leadership is perplexing and difficult. One has to determine whether leadership varies with the circumstances or whether there are similar principles of leadership exercised by leaders everywhere. Clearly, some people in authority are merely figureheads, while others manage to mobilize support for fundamental changes in the goals, institutions and culture of their organizations. The latter are the leaders — they are able to transcend the political system rather than merely survive it.

Most historians and political scientists would agree that leadership is one of the least understood social phenomena. Clearly, studies of leadership should encompass an understanding of the constraints and opportunities in politics. Writer Sidney Hook asked what makes an "event-making" person and concluded that the "hero" is someone who, by outstanding capacities of intelligence, will and character, determines an event or issue in a different way than if he had not acted. In other words, one must consider whether leadership is a necessary, if not a sufficient, condition to bring about the desired change.

How much do top political leaders shape events and how much are events merely instruments of other factors? Of course, all decisions of leaders are tempered by social conditions. But there is usually some room for leaders to manoeuvre — some margin of choice. The problem comes in assessing how much. It is difficult to specify what the outcome of a particular set of events would have been with or without the particular actor's intervention.

The "great man" theory that permeates much of the literature on Prime Ministers in Canada (at least while they are in office) errs in attributing too much choice to individuals, while neglecting the limitations which restrict the possibilities for action. On the other hand, the significance of leaders should not be undervalued either. Those who combine the required leadership traits have been able to leave a mark on history by their actions.

A survey of Canada's past Prime Ministers reveals a short list of those who are frequently called "great" leaders. Sir John A. Macdonald, Sir Wilfrid Laurier, Mackenzie King, Louis St. Laurent, Lester B. Pearson and Pierre Trudeau are among the handful who often receive high praise for their leadership qualities. All of them exhibited outstanding capacities of intelligence, will and character and did a great deal to determine the outcome of events in Canada.

Most of the seventeen Prime Ministers, however, are viewed merely as adequate or mediocre in terms of how they exercised the powers of office. On the whole, they were not able to rise to greatness themselves, or to inspire it in others. The few who were relative failures would have to include John Abbott, who at one time would have annexed Canada to the United States, Robert Borden, who divided the country with the First World War conscription debate, R.B. Bennett, who had the bad luck to be in power during the Depression, and John Diefenbaker, who won Quebec for the Conservatives and then ineptly alienated it in just a few years.

However, to Canada's credit, unlike the United States and many other democracies, this country has never yet placed a scoundrel or crook at the helm of government. All Prime Ministers have been honest, upright Canadians. That is not to say that none exhibited vulgar, bullying, or other downright unusual and colourful behaviour. Macdonald, a rather heavy drinker, once vomited in the House of Commons. On another memorable occasion he also threw up during a hustings platform debate with George Brown, but won over the audience with his comment, "The words of my worthy opponent have made me sick to my stomach." Mackenzie King communicated with his dead mother and seemed to be more fond of his dogs — all named "Pat" — than of anyone (except his mother). Trudeau was known to give hecklers and journalists "the finger," and once told westerners they had better vote for him or he wouldn't sell their wheat. John Abbott, who succeeded Sir John A. Macdonald from June 1891 to November 1892, came the closest to the "scoundrel" category of all the Prime Ministers. He was discovered to have signed an annexation manifesto several years earlier urging that Canada join the United States. Another serious accusation was that he was involved in delivering political kickbacks from the Canadian Pacific Railway to Sir John A. Macdonald in the Pacific Scandal of the 1870s.

ANALYZING LEADERSHIP

Leadership is multi-faceted. It is much more than the ability to win elections, essential though that is. Winning modern elections requires specific leadership attributes. But because these election-winning qualities tend to be very superficial, and are dwelt on *ad nauseam* by the media, they tend to distract from, or even be mistaken for, leadership ability.

Important electoral attributes in this country include oratorical ability, personal wealth, media presence, a photogenic family with philanthropic interests, good looks, fluent bilingualism, social graces, a relaxed manner and a modicum of sports ability. A leader may not have them all, but each one he or she does not have is considered to be a flaw for which compensation must be made.

Unfortunately, a leader can possess all these qualities, win elections, and still go down in history as a mediocre Prime Minister. They constitute the flashy, superficial qualities of show-biz which appeal to Canada's "media-ocracy." Electors, and particularly leadership convention delegates, need guidelines or clues which might help to determine which candidate, or candidates, have the "right stuff," apart from the ability to win elections.

There are several important qualities to look for in a leader. They can be summarized as a coherent vision for the country and executive talents to achieve the proposed goals and objectives. This combination of characteristics would enable a leader to decide what to do in any given circumstance and to get it done. Leaders need to project a clear and realistic view of where *they* would take the country in the next decade. They must be able to articulate how their vision for the country can be manifested in economic, social, constitutional and foreign affairs.

Few would dispute that a Prime Minister, in order to be considered a statesman and excellent leader, should have a blueprint or at least a vague national goal to provide the focus of government policies and politics. The vision, which may be based on a combination of judgment, instinct, circumstances and opportunities, must, in the light of history, be generally deemed appropriate and for the general good of the people. It must be a coherent and farsighted vision for the country and for the next generation of Canadians.

It is not enough to be a good communicator of words fed by overpaid speech writers. The leader must have something of substance to communicate, based on strong personal values and beliefs. In the 1988 election John Turner, leader of the Liberal Party, came alive and surprised and captivated the electorate when his deep convictions about Canada and the Tory Free Trade deal were communicated to his audiences. For the first time since becoming party leader his qualities were apparent to the electorate. Canadians should beware of the leader who has to be packaged and sold like soapflakes. Without a grasp of what is in the larger public interest, and the ability to persuade, party leaders cannot hope to bridge parochial divisions in the country and enlist public recognition and support.

Vision without executive talents in a Prime Minister is, of course, of little use either. If legislation cannot be passed, and circumstances cannot be dominated and shifted in the direction of the stated goal, then the leadership must be judged harshly. A leader must also have physical health, confidence and courage. A balance of common sense and imagination is needed as well as the ability to act decisively in a crisis.

We can flesh out these executive talents a little. Candidates who are prime ministerial material will possess a quick, flexible mind which will enable them to recognize and define fair compromises for difficult problems. As Ted Sorensen, speech writer for President John Kennedy, pointed out in a speech given at Geneva Park in January, 1987, "to govern is to choose — to choose among advice and advisers, between ends and means, principles and politics — and to choose intelligently, prudently and courageously. Effective political leadership is not a science but an art, requiring not calculation but judgment, not accurate measurements but wise choices." A leader

111

will be able to persuade, cajole, convince and even bully recalcitrants in the party and in the public at large into actively supporting, or at least passively going along with, the majority decision. This requires an ability to mobilize support by dominating the party, controlling the bureaucracy, cajoling the press and eventually convincing the public. A leader must shape public opinion and be prepared to confront popular positions in order to move toward his or her goals and vision. As Sorensen put it so wisely, leaders "must not yield to every popular passion and prejudice of the passing moment. They must offend some of the people in order to serve all of the people. And they must spend some popularity in order to serve all of the people." The most promising candidates are comfortable and self-confident in the role of initiator, so that they can capture and keep the initiative and dispel speculation and misinformation spread by rivals inside and outside the party.

A leader should also be a good administrator, interested in managing staff, budgets, organizational rules and the like, and must be able to raise the right questions and provide answers for them. A final indicator of a promising leader is the company of advisers on whom he or she relies for support and ideas. A team reveals a lot about a prospective leader's vision and ability to persuade. It can also demonstrate an ability to spot talent and manage individuals wisely. We should beware of the candidate who attracts only sycophants and yes-men. As great as an individual leader's executive talents may be, they will be of little avail if scandals, greed, petulance and corruption are in evidence among his or her allies. Outright enemies are sometimes easier to deal with than the unexpected weaknesses of those who are on the team.

Personality and Leadership

Personality traits affect a politician's behaviour and also the behaviour of others toward him or her. Ambition and a strong ego, for example, are often considered two important personality characteristics for those in public office. It is for this reason that personality development in youth is often studied to understand the development of political leaders.

Researchers are divided as to the extent to which personality is inherited or acquired, but they agree that both aspects are significant. Some writers claim that a specific type of personality is attracted to politics. Psychiatrists have postulated that political ambition and psychiatric disorders such as those found in the delusions of psychopaths, schizophrenics and paranoid personalities are related. Studies of Hitler and Stalin, for example, have been used to show that family background was instrumental in establishing personality disorders which affected their behaviour in later life. Erik H. Erikson argued that Hitler's disorders were due to the fact that he had failed to overcome his "crisis of adolescence" and develop an identity following his rejection by the Vienna Academy and the death of his mother. Erich Fromm argues that Hitler's afflictions were due to his narcissism — so that a natural relationship between Hitler and the external world never took place. And Robert Tucker, following the work on neurosis by Karen Horney, argues that Stalin developed a neurotic personality because of the beatings he endured from his father in the presence of his mother.

One social scientist, Harold Lasswell, emphasized that the desire to hold power over others is the prime motivation of politicians. They seek power as a compensation for feelings of inadequacy. According to this theory, politics brings on irrational behaviour as politicians strive for power to overcome low self-esteem. If these theories are valid, it would be important to explore the unconscious drives of Canadian Prime Ministers to determine if their personalities have in any way been distorted by their upbringing and early socialization.

Psycho-historical studies have also been made of Luther, Gandhi, Churchill and many others. The primary finding is that these individuals play out their private ambitions or personality needs on a large stage. Churchill has been described as someone searching for distinction because he was deprived of parental recognition and lacked self-esteem. Consequently, he was very aggressive and spent his life neurotically searching for a mission. President Woodrow Wilson, too, has been analyzed as being compulsive because of his relation to his father. Wilson is said to have resented his autocratic father but tried to live up to his ideals through his achievements which were always justified as moral.

There is considerable evidence that this thesis is exaggerated; not all leaders prove to be paranoid. However, there is more validity to the contention that particular personality types are drawn to politics: that individuals at the extreme ends of both high and low self-esteem enter politics. Many talented and successful leaders did not acquire major psychic scars in their youth. And different biographers often produce varying interpretations of the same person. One analyst finds a politician lacking in self-identity due to feelings of betrayal, guilt or anxiety, while another finds that the same subject was brought up in a family which, while not always comfortable, was nonetheless normal and not traumatic.

Pop historians tend to emphasize those parts of a person's personality that are congruent with later interpretations of their success or failure as politicians. If they are successful the positive traits, such as intelligence or diligence, are noticed. If, on the other hand, they are failures or remained in office only a short time, there is an effort to examine their early career for clues about their later problems.

It might be worthwhile to examine each Canadian Prime Minister's personality development to determine whether it had any effect on the success or failure of his career. Quite likely, one would find that personality factors have affected some Prime Ministers but not others. The problem is that much of the work in this field is drawn from biographies which are often inadequate, essentially descriptive and uncomparative. And there is usually a lack of evidence which forces the analyst to rely too heavily on theory and speculation. For this reason, historians and political scientists tend to rely on Prime Ministers' philosophies and actions to ascertain their motivations.

UP AND DOWN THE GREASY POLE

The position of Prime Minister is the most powerful and prestigious the Canadian political system has to offer. The Prime Minister wears many hats. Although he or she is not the Head of State, as is the American President, the position is the most important symbol of the federal government. The Prime Minister is chief executive officer, chief diplomat, chief legislator, chief of a political party, chief manager of the economy, the voice of Canadians, and Canada's leader on the world's stage.

Whoever holds this office heads the government, controls the majority of members of the House of Commons, commands a political party, assesses the careers of thousands of public servants, and can shine the light of publicity onto any public issue of his or her choosing. It is a heady responsibility, and clearly no individual would be able, in today's complex world, to do it alone. A Prime Minister must be able to achieve objectives through others. The choice of superbureaucrats, ministers and staff is perhaps the first critical job for a Prime Minister to tackle. Bad choices inevitably come home to roost as scandals or incompetence to weigh the leader down.

Much of this power is due to the position rather than the individual. Separating the office and the individual is a difficult task. It is not the inherent power itself but what the individual does with it that primarily concerns us here.

It is a rarified office. While today there are over 26 million Canadians, almost 300 are MPs, approximately 40 are Cabinet Ministers, and 10 are provincial Premiers. But there is only one Prime Minister. And the position does not change hands lightly. Since Confederation, only eighteen men have managed to climb the greasy pole and lay claim to the prize. Seven Liberals and eleven Conservatives have shared this top spot in the Canadian hierarchy. Four of the most adept perched there, holding others at bay, for a total of 71 years. John A. Macdonald, Sir Wilfrid Laurier, William Lyon Mackenzie King, and Pierre Elliot Trudeau dominated over half of all Canadian history. King held on the longest — twenty-two years — followed by Macdonald with twenty years, Trudeau with fifteen and a half and Laurier with fifteen consecutive years.

Table 4.1 Canada's Prime Ministers

Prime Minister	Dates of Administration
Sir John A. Macdonald	1 Jul. 1867 - 5 Nov. 1873 17 Oct. 1878 - 6 June 1891
Alexander Mackenzie	7 Nov. 1873 - 9 Oct. 1878
Sir John Abbott	16 June 1891 - 24 Nov. 1892
Sir John Thompson	5 Dec. 1892 - 12 Dec. 1894
Sir Mackenzie Bowel	21 Dec. 1894 - 27 April 1896
Sir Charles Tupper	1 May - 8 July, 1986
Sir Wilfrid Laurier	11 July 1896 - 6 Oct. 1911
Sir Robert L. Borden	10 Oct. 1911 - 10 July 1920
Arthur Meighen	10 Jul. 1920 - 29 Dec. 1921 29 June 1926 - 25 Sept. 1926
W. L. Mackenzie King	29 Dec. 1921 - June 28 1926 25 Sept. 1926 - 6 Aug. 1930 23 Oct. 1935 - 15 Nov. 1948
Richard B. Bennett	7 Aug. 1930 - 23 Oct. 1935
Louis St. Laurent	15 Nov. 1948 - 21 June 1957
John G. Diefenbaker	21 June 1957 - 22 Apr. 1963
Lester B. Pearson	22 Apr. 1963 - 20 Apr. 1968
Pierre Elliott Trudeau	20 Apr. 1968 - 4 June 1979 3 Mar. 1980 - 30 June 1984
Charles Joseph Clark	4 June 1979 - 3 Mar. 1980
John Napier Turner	30 June - 17 Sept. 1984
Martin Brian Mulroney	17 Sept. 1984 -

A few PMs slid back down almost as soon as they had arrived; others held on for a few years. The shortest careers were those of Thompson, Abbott, Bowell, Tupper, Clark and Turner all of whom served for less than two years. Borden, St. Laurent, Mackenzie, Bennett, Diefenbaker and Pearson held on for between five and eleven years.

In a democracy the reigning myth is that anyone, no matter how humble his or her origin, may become Prime Minister. It has been said that "Macdonald showed a Prime Minister can be poor; Trudeau showed a Prime Minister can be rich; Clark showed it doesn't matter who is Prime Minister; and Mulroney showed the country could be better off without a Prime Minister." Be that as it may, several early Prime Ministers, it is true, were from extremely humble backgrounds. But circumstances have changed; the frontier society is well behind us, and only the supremely naive believe that aspiration matches opportunity in Canada today. There are, however, a great many characteristics that our Prime Ministers have shared, characteristics that developed very early in life.

Prime Ministers, and all politicians in the western world, are atypical of their fellow citizens. In general, they tend to be an ambitious lot, gregarious, informed individuals who possess a strong confidence in their abilities. Drawn from the higher socio-economic groups, they also tend to be male, middle-class, middle-aged and well educated. Some professions such as law, business, teaching and journalism tend to be over-represented in the ranks of elected politicians. This creates an unrepresentative elite which is easily accused of producing policies which are favourable to certain groups in society, or which structure specific predispositions toward social conflict.

Prime Ministers evince all of these characteristics, but in many cases the qualities are even more refined. These few, select individuals tend to be even better educated wealthier and better connected to the social and economic elite of the country than their elected colleagues. And, of course, to date all have been male.

Political participation can be viewed as a giant pyramid. Forming the base are the multitude of Canadians who participate infrequently — generally just at election time, or not at all. Most individuals at this level of the pyramid are not university educated and hold labour or blue-collar type jobs. At each successive level of the pyramid, as political participation becomes more intense, educational and socio-economic qualifications tend to increase while the number of individuals decreases.

While elected politicians form a relatively small elite group near the top of the pyramid, cabinet ministers constitute an even smaller elite, and, of course, the Prime Minister is at the apex. It would be the very rare individual indeed who started at the bottom of the pyramid and ended up reaching the top. Almost without exception, our Prime Ministers were raised in an environment which encouraged political participation and most often, though not always, in above-average financial circumstances so that they could afford to be concerned with politics rather than economic survival. In this setting they developed the interest, motivation and skills which are necessary to succeed in political life.

Politicians who make it to the top of the greasy pole tend to have other fairly similar characteristics. The average age for attaining this office is 56. Joe Clark was the youngest at 39, but he hung on for less than a year. Since the First World War every Prime Minister has been not only a university graduate, but has graduated from law or graduate school as well.

How are the careers of Prime Ministers terminated? Given the stress of the position one might suppose that they would simply tire of office. But, in fact, very few have retired of their own choice. Eleven were defeated in a general election (one was kicked out in a cabinet revolt, two through defeats in Parliament) and two died in office. In other words, only five chose to retire of their own accord.

118

Moreover, getting rid of Prime Ministers is very difficult. Two-thirds of Prime Ministers who decided to contest an election while in office managed to get returned to office again.

Given the importance of Prime Ministers to the economic and social well-being of Canadians, one would think that it is vital to make the right choice of leader and that the utmost care would be taken in leadership selection. Unfortunately that is not the case. Since the primary goal of parties is to win elections, party militants tend to concentrate on the wrong qualities; they want someone who is media-friendly. There is not nearly enough emphasis on whether a candidate has a coherent vision and executive talents.

Cartoon character Charlie Brown once opined that there is no heavier burden than a great potential. The winner of a party leadership convention could become Prime Minister and be called on to demonstrate much more leadership than just electoral prowess. Perhaps those who attend leadership conferences should score candidates on two checklists — one which highlights attributes needed to win elections and another which recognizes leadership qualities.

PRIME MINISTERS AND VISION

Canada's first seventeen Prime Ministers were leaders of two different political parties, but in three important areas they held basically the same conception about how the country should be governed. First, they shared a vision in which the federal government would be the major actor in the constitutional, economic and social life of the country. They knew that "where there is no vision, the people perish" (Proverbs 29:18 — inscribed on the west arch of the Peace Tower, Ottawa). While a few accepted a modest degree of decentralization on occasion, they all acted as guardians of the national interest. They conceived of the country in terms of something greater than the provinces, ethnic groups and special interests within it. All tended to think the greatest task for leadership was "national unity" which, on the whole, meant reconciliation of the diverse interests in the country.

Secondly, all past Prime Ministers acted as if they believed in a mildly interventionist state which would act, whenever necessary, for the economic development of the country. None of them accepted the argument that "market forces" alone could keep the country together and prosperous. They all saw some role for the state to mitigate the harsh realities of raw market economics.

Thirdly, all seventeen conceived that the government had to provide a social safety net for the less fortunate or less able members of society. In other words, they believed in the capacity of the federal government to both solve problems of economic growth and promote social justice.

Every Prime Minister of Canada, until Brian Mulroney, has believed and acted on these three assumptions about governance in Canada. They knew — as the Fathers of Confederation knew when theyb brought the colonies together — that a strong central government would be required to balance a country composed of French and English, Protestants and Catholics.

State action to bolster the economy was also taken for granted from Confederation on. Macdonald's National Policy consisted of a mixture of high tariffs to protect new industries and railway-building to open up the West to commerce. Over time Conservative and Liberal Prime Ministers helped to build railway and airline transportation systems to bind the country together. Later, the Canadian Broadcasting Corporation was created to link the country through communications.

Together, Conservative and Liberal Prime Ministers and their governments created a social safety net that is one of the best in the world, beginning with old age pensions and family allowances and proceeding through unemployment insurance, welfare assistance and finally, in 1966, to universal medicare. Successive Prime Ministers have added incrementally to these so that today Canada possesses a comprehensive social policy that serves the needs of all its citizens. Social justice is also provided by the federal government's ability to transfer money to poorer provinces through equalization grants, allowing less affluent areas of the country to maintain adequate levels of public services.

The first five Prime Ministers to follow Macdonald did little but continue to build the country on his policy coat-tails. Liberal Alexander Mackenzie did help to create the Northwest Mounted Police — which was to become the famed Mounties who helped in the generally peaceful opening up of the West. The four Conservatives who followed as Prime Minister — Abbott, Thompson, Bowell and Tupper — lasted only five years in total, from 1891 to 1896. Their combined effect was to set the stage for the arrival of the great conciliator, Sir Wilfrid Laurier, who was to govern from 1896 to 1911.

Once in office Laurier devoted himself to reconciling English and French. He put "Canadianism" ahead of both ethnic groups. He completed Macdonald's work of state-building by adding Saskatchewan and Alberta to Confederation and overseeing Canadian expansion as far as Yukon. It was the latter event which gave rise to his famous quotation that "The twentieth century belongs to Canada."

Canada's eighth and ninth Prime Ministers were Conservatives. And yet they set about to extend government activity in the private sector. Sir Robert Borden is best known for his activities in the First World War and for getting Canada into the League of Nations. But Sir Robert was also responsible for the nationalization of the Canadian Northern Railway, a major step toward the creation of the Canadian National Railway. Arthur Meighen followed Borden in this task. He nationalized several private transportation companies to complete the construction of the CNR.

William Lyon Mackenzie King retained power for the longest period of any Prime Minister. Dominating Canadian politics from the 1920s to the end of the Second World War, King was best known for his temporizing on matters of public policy. As he put it: "In politics one has to do as one at sea in a sailing ship; not try to go straight ahead but reach one's course having regard to the prevailing winds." But it was King who began Canada's modern social policies by driving through the first old age pension scheme in 1927.

Later, after Conservative Prime Minister R.B. Bennett tried and failed to obtain court agreement for a national employment insurance program (Employment and Social Insurance Act), it was King again who sought and received a constitutional amendment so that Canada's first comprehensive unemployment insurance scheme could be implemented. Bennett also introduced the Broadcast Act of 1932 which fostered the policy of public ownership — a policy which was to flourish and lead to the Canadian Broadcasting Corporation in 1936 under Mackenzie King. And King was Prime Minister when Trans-Canada Airlines was set up in 1937. It became Air Canada in 1965 under Lester B. Pearson.

Louis St. Laurent continued the work of strengthening the social security net for Canadians by adding the *Old Age Security Act* which provided extra income for seniors in financial need. He was also in power when the trans-Canada pipeline was built to bring western oil and gas to central Canada. While pressure for a national highway began as early as 1910, it was Prime Minister St. Laurent who joined with the provinces to finally build the trans-Canada highway.

Conservative Prime Minister John Diefenbaker fostered a new era of state-building with his "northern vision" which inspired greater awareness of Canada's vast northern regions. Lester B. Pearson, the statesman, completed the process of state building by raising Canada's image abroad, adding a Canadian flag, and giving Canada its first nation-wide medicare plan. Clark and Turner did not have enough time in office to add to the three-fold structure of the Canadian state.

Like all the Prime Ministers before him, Pierre Trudeau carried on the tradition of state-building, imposing the federal government on the economy from time to time and reinforcing the social security net. Moreover, he articulated these goals in terms of a pan-Canadian vision which consisted of a bilingual and multicultural country led by a strong central government with a social conscience. His philosophy of economic intervention was evident in the creation of the National Energy Program, the Foreign Investment Review Agency, Via Rail and Petro-Canada. But it is in the constitutional field that Trudeau will be remembered most.

The catalyst to Trudeau's action on the Constitution, and his most important legacy, was the defeat of the 1980 Quebec referendum on sovereignty-association. Federal opponents of this proposal — led by Trudeau — pledged during the campaign that Canada would begin a process of "constitutional renewal" if Quebeckers rejected the referendum. The concept of "renewal" allowed Trudeau to revive his efforts to patriate the Canadian Constitution, a goal which he had set during his first election as Prime Minister in 1968. After intense federal-provincial bargaining, machinations of the British Parliament, and inconclusive decisions by the Supreme Court, the federal government and nine provinces finally settled on a constitutional deal. It included patriation — the symbolic assertion that the Constitution was made in Canada, not Britain — a set of amendment formulae, and a *Charter of Rights and Freedoms* to protect citizens against the state.

Only the Quebec government did not sign the constitutional deal. But the federal government went ahead anyway. Separatists spread the myth that Quebec had been humiliated. At this juncture in Canadian history Pierre Elliot Trudeau resigned. He was replaced by John Turner who promptly called a general election in 1984 only to be defeated by the Conservatives led by Brian Mulroney.

Of course, leaders of the official opposition can provide important contributions to the debate about public policy. Joe Clark did this by confronting Trudeau's vision of one Canada with his own view that Canada was a "community of communities." John Turner, too, made his contribution. Over two years before the November 1988 general election, John Turner, on a slow walk behind the parliament buildings, said privately to me, "Bob, if you can just get me to the free trade debate with Mulroney I can win the election." Two years of policy development then went into the decision that John Turner would ask the Senate to block the Free Trade Agreement and cause a general election. (The final tactic to say that Turner would "rip up the deal" was made in a secret meeting between Turner, the chief of staff, the legislative adviser and myself as senior policy adviser. While I supported the anti-free-trade position, I opposed the emotive language of "rip up." In the end the legislative adviser won over Mr. Turner by his partisan comment that if the Liberals did not say they would rip it up, then the NDP would outflank them on the negative approach to the deal.)

Mulroney also had a vision of Canada when he came to power. But it was a very different one from Trudeau's and all other preceding Prime Ministers, based on a neo-conservative philosophy of small government and the importance of private enterprise and improving Canada's economic competitiveness. Constitutionally, Mulroney has become the most decentralizing Prime Minister in Canadian history. Setting out to right the so-called wrong over Quebec's "humiliation" by the 1982 constitutional amendments, he has led the country to near constitutional chaos. His government, whether deliberately or not, has begun to dismantle the three pillars of federal government activity (strong central government, responsible participation in the economy and universal social programs) which have been the cornerstones of the Canadian federation from 1867 to 1984, and which were defended and added to by all previous Prime Ministers regardless of party affiliation. Mr. Mulroney has shifted the entire dialogue of politics in Canada in two respects: from a debate over centre-left philosophies to one over conservative versus arch-conservative ideas; and from one over the appropriate constitutional balance to one about how to decentralize the country.

Canada has not had the kind of leadership it deserves from a good number of its Prime Ministers. But, prior to Brian Mulroney, all of them have undertaken to lead the country from the perspective of a strong activist federal government. In the very short time since the Conservatives came to power in 1984 we have gone from a prosperous and forward-looking country to a fractious group of interests. The 21st century could still belong to Canada. But not without firm leadership. Canadians today believe leadership is sadly lacking.

THE CREDIBILITY FACTOR

Currently, the conflicting claims of various interests are raging out of control like a pack of yapping dogs nipping at the government's heels. Politicians cannot control the situation and populism has been on the rise. Canadians used to regard politics more like the Victorians regarded sex — as something necessary, but rather vulgar — and certainly not to be enjoyed by ladies. That is no longer the case. Everybody today, it seems, has a cause and supports a group to help fight for it on the political scene. Government is in disrepute, and one-issue interest groups are both contributing to and benefiting from widespread dissatisfaction with government.

Most Canadians agree that authoritative leadership is absolutely vital to make and carry out difficult decisions during times of crisis. Only a strong leader backed by a new mandate can bridge the wide regional and ethnic divisions in this country. As usual when things go badly, the Prime Minister attracts the brunt of the scorn. Some of the deep cynicism and discontent which Brian Mulroney has attracted can be attributed to this general malaise and tetchiness. In the spring of 1992, eight years after Pierre Trudeau had retired to a quiet life in Montreal, two Environics surveys found that Canadians still believed he had the best leadership abilities to handle constitutional problems.

Discontent, Populism, and Weak Leadership

It is a paradox that voters in Canada turn out regularly at election time — about 70% vote — yet a majority of them is personally dissatisfied. As one resigned voter put it, "no matter who you vote for a politician always gets in." Canadians are democrats at heart; they think they can vote their way out of problems. They are relatively satisfied immediately after the election, but that is only temporary — disillusionment sets in very rapidly.

Figure 4:1 Support of the Government Party Gallup Results % of Total and Inter-Election Trends

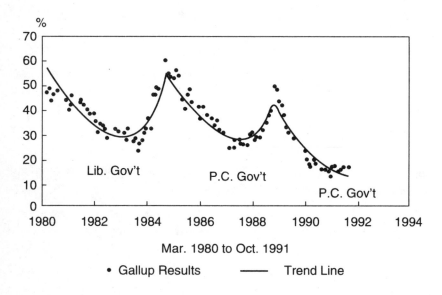

Mar. 1980 to Oct. 1991

• Gallup Results　　　——　Trend Line

Popularity for Mr. Mulroney's party and government went into free fall shortly after both the 1984 and 1988 elections. Support for the government party in the spring of 1992 was the lowest that Gallup had discovered in the last decade. Gallup found that the Conservatives would obtain only 16% of the vote if an election were held at that time. Disillusionment with the government is particularly deep, but the erosion in Conservative support matches the continual erosion in support for *all* governments, both Liberal and Conservative, during the past two decades.

While the press pays extraordinary attention to the Prime Minister's lack of popularity, he is not the only target of discontent in the country. Dissatisfaction with political leaders has expanded to encompass a crisis of confidence in institutions. Government *per se* is beginning to lack legitimacy. As Peter Dobell and Bryon Berry put it, "Canadian political discontent is at its highest since polling began."

In Canada, as in other industrialized democracies, there is a declining confidence in political institutions. None of the major institutions, Parliament, political parties or the federal government, command respect. As for the House of Commons itself, Gallup poll data from 1974-1990 shows a continual decline in Canadian respect for that institution. Respect for political parties has dropped from 18% to only 9% as of March 1992. The following polls on respect and confidence tell the story.

There is no doubt that Canadians are angry and frustrated with politicians. Members of Parliament have especially low popularity. Gallup's survey of the honesty and ethical standards of MPs in 1989 ranked them 11th of 12 professions, below labour unions and building contractors.

André Blais and Elizabeth Gidengil also found discontent to be at a historically high level in Canada. Measuring six variables they discovered that 49% of Canadians do not trust the federal government and 52% believe that "quite a few of the people running the government are a little bit crooked."

Two government commissions have also confirmed a high degree of discontent and lack of confidence in politicians and institutions. The Citizen's Forum on Canada's Future (the Spicer Commission) and the Royal Commission on Electoral Reform and Party Financing both showed an extreme lack of confidence and public discontent. Both of them witnessed an outpouring of criticism that Canada lacked responsible leadership, that current leaders were not trustworthy and that the country lacked strong leaders. Of course some of this anger is due to the fact that a majority of Canadians dislike the Free Trade deal with the United States and the Goods and Service Tax. But it is the present government which has given us those policies as well as attempting to decentralize the country, reduce government involvement in the economy and put holes in the social security net. This government is led by Brian Mulroney.

Figure 4:2 National Institutions 1990

Levels of Public Respect and Confidence

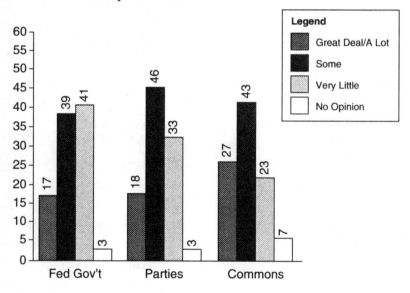

SOURCE: Gallup Reports, 4 Jun/90 and 17 Sept/90

Figure 4:3 National Institutions 1979-1992

High Respect and Confidence

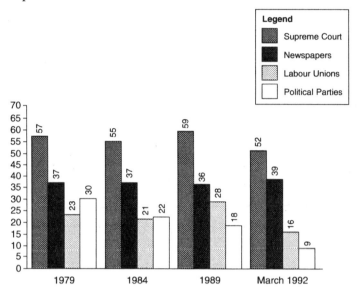

SOURCE: Gallup Report, 16 March 1992.

*Respondents were asked to rate how much respect and confidence they had for the insti-
tution listed. Scores are for those who answered "A Great Deal" or "A Lot", as opposed to "Some" or "No Opinion."*

Media-ocracy

Television plays a significant role in creating public cynicism and
dissatisfaction with politicians. As a mediator between government
and the people, it is a major player in the democratic process. It is the
main source of information for most Canadians and the chief means
of communication between those who govern and the populace. It
selects what and whom will receive time on air and the length of
exposure. In the past 20 years, on-air-time television clips of politicians have declined drastically to about five to seven seconds per

appearance. Communication has been reduced to meaningless slogans and simple-minded phrases.

Figure 4:4 House of Commons

Respect and Confidence, 1974-1990

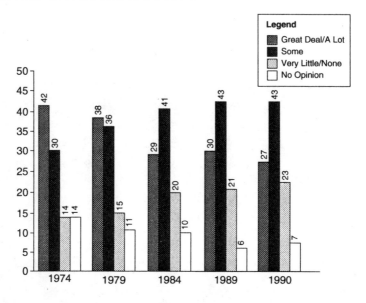

SOURCE: Gallup Reports Sept/74, Aug/79, Jan/85, Feb/89, Jun/90

Television is episodic rather than process oriented. It presents the news in tiny segments with little, if any, continuous analysis of what events mean. It is like watching a movie one frame at a time; we never get to understand the story line. What we see is not the valuable effects of governing, law-making or the distribution of economic resources, but instead Brian Mulroney's jaw and gravelly voice, Mila's perky smile and fresh hairdo, Jean Chrétien's heavy accent, Audrey McLaughlin's bright jacket, Manning's reverential platitudes, Parizeau's pompous grin.

Government has become an enormous public relations exercise. Some personal experiences make this clear. As a legislative adviser during the Trudeau Cabinet I once was handed a note by a senior cabinet minister that said, "As a former professor of political science I agree with everything you have just said — but as a politician I don't think we should do any of it." In another incident, while senior policy adviser to the Liberal Party, I volunteered to go to the television studio with John Turner. A senior party hatchet man asked if I would tell the truth or lie to the journalists. When I replied that I would only tell the truth, he responded, "Then you're no spin doctor. You can't go."

Figure 4:5 Political Corruption

Percent Believing Many Politicians are Crooked

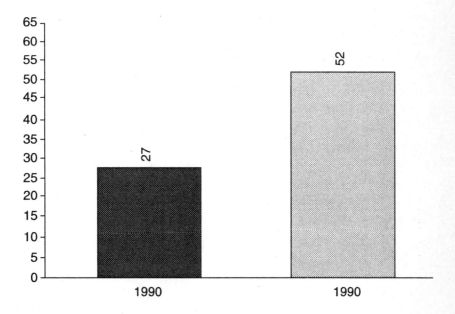

SOURCE: André Blais and Elizabeth Gidengil, "Representative Democracy: The Views of Canadians, 1991, "Royal Commission on Electoral Reform and Party Financing, *Reforming Electoral Democracy*, vol 1 (Ottawa: Supply and Services, 1992) p. 225

Public cynicism is predictable given roughly 40 years of the media distorting and trivializing events. It has conditioned viewers to be indifferent to elected officials and helped convince them that they have no voice in politics. And when the media interpret politicians' behaviour they give the impression that politicians engage in obscure incantations and act out unfathomable customs. Often there are distortions in order to make an event newsworthy. This was the point of the well known joke about John Turner's uphill battle for media recognition. One night, it is said, his aid looked out the window on Parliament Hill and saw Turner pacing back and forth on the Ottawa River. "This is amazing," he thought, "wait till the reporters see he can walk on water." He summoned them. They watched as Turner walked all the way to Hull and back on the river. The next day the newspaper headlines read, "John Turner can't swim!"

Knowing this kind of distortion takes place regularly will give little consolation to the Prime Minister and his fellow politicians as they try to re-establish their credibility. There is a relationship between credibility and trust. Public opinion polls indicate that on the whole politicians are not liked, not believed, not trusted and not respected. It is a sad commentary on political leadership. Citizens go through the motions of elections, but find that scandals involving conflict of interest, blatant greed and misuse of taxpayers' money lead them to expect the worst of their politicians.

BEYOND CYNICISM

The first step away from the long, soul-destroying debate over the future of Canada is to break free of today's cyncism. Canadians need a leader who is able to restore their faith in political institutions and leaders and in the democratic process. Until such a person is in power, prosperity and political stability will be little more than a fond memory of days gone by.

Canadians are facing a period of political crisis. Arthur Schlesinger, Jr., studying how Presidents in the United States have acted in times of crisis, said that Franklin Roosevelt made it possible for people to believe again in government's capacity to solve problems of economic stability and social justice. Canada needs just such a leader. Today's problems require a Prime Minister who can firmly and calmly reject the falsehoods that parade as facts in discussions of constitutional change; someone to remind Canadians how fortunate they are, to defend the country's heritage, and to find ways to reinforce the spiritual bonds that hold this huge, diverse country together. Canadians need someone to clarify the language of political debate and prevent the misunderstandings that drive them apart. These things must be done on a regular basis, not only at election time or on Canada Day or when the situation has deteriorated to the point of holding referendums on whether or not the country will remain united. Where is the leader who will renew Lester B. Pearson's stirring pledge "to excite the daring, test the strong and give promise to the timid"?

5 Brian Mulroney: The Father Of Constitutional Disintegration?

"You've got covert action, prejudice to extremes
You've got primitive cunning and high tech means
You've got eyes everywhere, but people see through you"

—From People See Through You
by Bruce Cockburn

Brian Mulroney swept to power in 1984 with more seats in the House of Commons than any other Tory leader in Canadian history. Eight years later he is still Prime Minister, but his popularity has reached a record low. Public opinion polls for the first half of 1992 lingered disapprovingly around 11% before they edged up slightly. Apart from a temporary blip around the 1988 election, and what may be another one building in late 1992, there has been a steady decline in the Prime Minister's approval rates and a corresponding increase in disapproval rates since 1984. In politics it is a short road from giddy triumph to despair.

Another election is due before November 1993. As a master of the electoral count-down and roll of the dice, Prime Minister Mulroney is aware that collective memory is very short indeed and that public opinion can change radically from year to year. Despite the fact that he has brought the country to the brink of disaster with policies which weaken the federal government, it is within the realm of possibility that the Conservatives will be re-elected in 1993. If, however, as is becoming increasingly likely, Canadians splinter their vote and put in power a weak minority government with five parties sharing the parliamentary seats, it is uncertain who will become Prime Minister. It could be such a stalemated government that it will hardly matter.

For most of his two terms in office Mr. Mulroney has lacked the legitimacy to represent the country as a whole. Canadians no longer believe what "lyin' Brian" says. Persuasive speeches and policy pronouncements about the country fall on deaf ears. One formerly loyal Conservative simply says, "I turn the TV off whenever Mulroney comes on." Mulroney partisans say he has been the lightning rod for all the discontent in the country. But that is only part of the reason for his unpopularity.

Figure 5:1 The Prime Minister

Percent Approving of Mulroney as P.M.

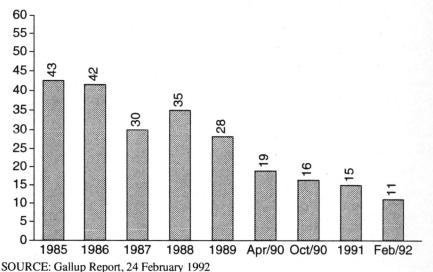

SOURCE: Gallup Report, 24 February 1992

There are several factors that account for this high public disillusionment. They include a general skepticism about politics; the fact that Mr. Mulroney has been in office for two terms and has worn off a great deal of his gloss; his tendency to use exaggeration and hyperbole without being able to follow through; his penchant for accepting and trying to exploit the ideology of difference; and lastly, the simple fact that Canadian Prime Ministers, in comparison with others around the world, often have a low popularity rating due to regional divisions in the country. It is difficult to placate all Canadian interests in any dispute, let alone one as fundamental as the viability of the country.

Mr. Mulroney does have the two requisites of political leadership — vision and executive talents. But he has used those talents to weaken the federal government in the apparent belief that the government should not interfere with the market forces or provide an appropriate social policy for the country. Thoughtful Canadians ask why a Conservative government which led us to war in the Persian Gulf and forced through the hated GST and Free Trade Agreement has given such poor leadership on questions which threaten the country's stability and viability. On economic, social and constitutional problems Conservative policies have brought the country to the brink of disintegration.

The Prime Minister's popularity was so low, due to the FTA, the GST, Meech Lake and general constitutional malaise, that the following "Canadian Test" joke flourished in early 1991, coinciding with the Gulf War and the implementation of the GST:

Question: You're locked in a room with Saddam Hussein, Yassar Arafat and Brian Mulroney. You've got a gun and two bullets. What do you do?

Answer: Shoot Mulroney twice — you *don't* want to miss.

For normally gentle, peace-loving Canadians this was an untypical and fairly violent expression of sentiment towards the political head of government.

THE MULRONEY CHARACTER

As we determined in Chapter 4, relating the personality characteristics of leaders to their actions can shed light on public policy — although all such claims should be made modestly. Biographers, particularly John Sawatsky, have provided a rich source of material about Brian Mulroney. In Sawatsky's recent book, *The Politics of Ambition*, we can find some clues from Mulroney's formative years about the choices he makes as Prime Minister. Some are worth mentioning.

Probably the best known story documenting the formation of young Brian's attitudes toward the United States relates how Colonel Robert McCormick, owner of the *Chicago Tribune* and *New York Daily News*, regularly visited Mulroney's home town of Baie Comeau. On each occasion, Mr. McCormick hired Mulroney to sing for him and rewarded the boy with a US $50 bill. These visits were very significant events for the young boy from a large, modest-income family. It does not take much imagination to find parallels between this deeply ingrained behaviour and Mulroney's positive relationship with the United States today.

The young Mulroney manifested his drive for politics early. He had a strong belief in himself and was extraordinarily tenacious. He was also pragmatic and quite willing to adapt his political goals in order to win. When he first arrived at St. Francis Xavier University, for example, he wanted to become involved in campus politics as a Liberal. It was part of his family tradition; the Liberals were the natural party of a Catholic, lower-middle-class Quebecker at that time, and it was the most popular party on the St. FX campus. But instead, Mulroney joined the Conservatives where his personal chances were more propitious. He soon became leader of the campus PC Party and dreamed of repeating the Diefenbaker miracle of uprooting the arrogant Liberals in the Model Parliament. He found he loved campaigning and was outstandingly good at it.

After graduating from Laval Law School, Mr. Mulroney became a lawyer specializing in labour law. That job appears to have taught him that any deal is better than no deal. He learned to act on the principle that if a deal has some weaknesses it is not a big problem because losses can be recouped at the next set of negotiations. He also learned the tactics of "pressure cooker" bargaining which produces agreement by exhaustion.

Mulroney's highest executive position before becoming Prime Minister was President of the Iron Ore Company of Canada, a subsidiary of a US Corporation. His major responsibility at the mine seems to have been to lay off workers and close down the mining town of Schefferville. This experience and a hard-nosed quality have served him well as a Prime Minister whose economic policies have forced plant closures and hard times across the country.

Throughout his adult political career, Mulroney has shown the same pragmatism, persistence and outstanding campaign qualities that he had at university. Mulroney began as a "red Tory" but shifted to the right for strategic and tactical reasons. He needed the right wing of the Conservative Party to help him dislodge the hapless Prime Minister Joe Clark. Again, with a keen eye for a vote, he joined forces with nationalists who helped him win the 1984 election in Quebec. However, this placed him in the hands of strong nationalists in his cabinet and caucus.

THE MULRONEY VISION

Brian Mulroney has developed a vision for Canada, but it is decidedly different from those of earlier Prime Ministers. His neo-conservative polices have increased tensions along ethnic and regional fault lines. Mr. Mulroney sometimes gives lip service to the time-tried vision of a strong, united country with a social conscience, but in practice he follows a different path.

After his election in 1984 one of the first things the new Mulroney government did was table its economic policy, "A New Direction for Canada: An Agenda for Economic Renewal." It was a right-wing policy document which declared Canada to be in an economic crisis. According to this document, the priority of the new government would be to reduce the national debt, annual deficits and the activities of federal government. In view of the fact that the old mixed economy had failed, it said, the government would give priority to creating a smaller, decentralized, deregulated system. It would attempt to enhance a market-force economy and privatize government holdings wherever possible. In other words, the government would commit itself to a free-enterprise philosophy akin to those followed by Ronald Reagan in the United States and by Margaret Thatcher in the United Kingdom.

Eventually this philosophy led to cuts in social programs. When Mulroney began his career as leader of the Conservative Party he was in favour of Canada's social program, declaring that they were a "social trust." Once in power he became the exponent of gross free-enterprise conservatism. His government set out to weaken or destroy old-age pensions, unemployment insurance, family allowances, public housing, welfare payments (by capping payments to provinces), and even medicare. The same direction was taken in increasing privatization of services and facilities provided by Ottawa (Via Rail being a prime case) and in the attack on universality as a basis for disbursing federal government benefits and services in all fields. The government also reduced payments under the Established Programs Financing Act for health-care and post-secondary education.

The best known of these Conservative policies was to reduce the indexation of old-age pensions. During a "grey power" rally to protest the move, one old age pensioner captured the mood of her cohorts on Parliament Hill when she told Mulroney: "You lied to us. You got us to vote for you and then — it's good-bye, Charlie Brown." These reductions have been mostly at the expense of the poor; a very large proportion of those losing benefits are low-income workers earning less than $25,000 a year.

The vision was implemented even further after the 1988 election with the unpopular Goods and Service Tax (GST) and the Free Trade Agreement (FTA) with the United States. The GST eroded the progressiveness of the tax system. As a consumption tax, it is regressive because every person pays the same amount on a purchase regardless of their level of income. The Free Trade deal reduces Canada's ability to make independent decisions over energy, natural resources, social policy, environmental protection, consumer protection standards and culture.

These policies in their composite have weakened the federal government's ability to provide services equally to all Canadians and to speak for Canada abroad with one strong voice. There is no doubt that Mulroney's policies are based on a neo-conservative vision which is accepted with open arms by the business community. "Small c" conservative ideology is, essentially, to abandon traditional patterns of governance in Canada and move rapidly toward a "minimalist state" and a "laissez-faire" philosophy based on American, rather than Canadian, culture. As a new economic and political philosphy it underlies a general retreat from governance.

The money cut from such social spending was needed, according to the Conservative government, to help pay down the country's $440 billion public debt which is costing Canadians 36 cents out of every tax dollar collected for interest payments alone. The impact of this astonishing figure can be reduced somewhat if the deficits and surpluses of the various provincial budgets are included to give a more complete picture of the country's financial state. The interest on the debt of all eleven governments combined is 22 cents on the tax dollar. It is also wise to remember that about 60% of the debt is held by Canadians and thus interest payments on it are going right back into their pockets. But it is also the case that an increasing proportion of the national debt is foreign controlled and this is a dangerous situation.

The Tory message is clear, persuasive and worrisome: Canadians are spending more than they are earning, and something must be done to eliminate the deficits and debt. The figures are so large as to be meaningless to ordinary Canadians, but the tangible results of this drain on the economy are evident to all.

The public debt must be reduced. But paying it down should not be used to justify deep cuts in social spending which has actually moderated as a percentage of Gross Domestic Product since 1975, the same period during which the $440 billion debt accumulated. A country should be judged by how it takes care of the weakest in its society — the poor, the handicapped and the least fortunate. Their meagre resources should not be in the front line to pay the national debt run up by the rich and powerful.

There are currently two fairly distinct economic visions of Canada competing for support: one led by Brian Mulroney is based on the belief that a smaller, less activist government will somehow make Canada more competitive and thus more prosperous, and another, which posits that enhanced government services and a strong federal government are increasingly required to make Canada successful in the new global economy.

It is vital for Canadians to decide which of these visions they want for Canada and to understand what their decision entails. This fundamental debate over the role of government in Canada should be a major consideration at the next general election. But what concerns us in this volume is that Conservative constitutional proposals such as the Meech Lake and Charlottetown accords also adhere to the principle of retreat from federal government responsibilities.

THE CONSTITUTIONAL ISSUES

The major test of leadership in the Mulroney years, overriding even the serious economic concerns, has been constitutional reform. The constitutional issue is not new; it has been around for at least two and a half decades. In the mid 1960s, under Prime Minister Lester Pearson's government, an early attempt to patriate the Constitution failed. Pearson accommodated Quebec, but did not patriate or change the Constitution. In 1971, the Victoria Charter was negotiated and then scuttled at the last moment by Quebec Premier Robert Bourassa. Trudeau tried again throughout the 1970s, but failed to get agreement. Then, in 1982, Mr. Trudeau's patriation package was implemented without the support of the separatist government of Quebec. It was the only composite major constitutional deal since 1867 to survive beyond the early stages.

Brian Mulroney did not, then, introduce the general problem of constitutional reform in Canada. But he is responsible for the escalating tensions, setting Canadian against Canadian to the point where the country may disintegrate over it. What began as the fulfillment of a promise by Pierre Trudeau to "renew" the federal bargain and make adjustments so that Quebec would sign the Constitution has ended as a full-scale national crisis involving Quebec, aboriginal and regional fault lines. Ironically, it all began when Prime Minister Mulroney's first Speech from the Throne in 1984 declared that his government would bring the country "national reconciliation."

What should have been a fairly simple process — Quebec's Premier Bourassa only had five modest requests — turned into complicated constitutional negotiations which resemble a many-headed hydra. The process has been so inflammatory and so debilitating for the government that today it seems willing to saddle the country with an unworkable, divisive and ramshackle system simply in order to get an agreement — any agreement.

To a large extent, Mulroney is personally responsible for the chain of events which fueled the flames of separatism in Quebec, regionalism in the West and aboriginal demands. His penchant for strategies which allow problems to fester and grow, and then to set sudden deadlines and gamble on the outcome, has been successful electorally for the Tories, but a disaster for Canada.

Mulroney introduced the Meech Lake reforms, and using his bargaining skills and pressure cooker tactics cobbled together a package that had more to do with making different interests happy than it did with building a strong, prosperous and united Canada. The package exploded. The story is familiar, but some highlights are worth reviewing because already myths are distorting history; selective memory, blind spots and creative embellishment are taking over.

It should not be forgotten that Mulroney supported Trudeau's patriation of the Constitution in 1982. That was before Mulroney made deals with nationalists and separatists in the province of Quebec in his effort to win his home province in the 1984 election. After the victory he included nationalists such as Marcel Masse as well as the turncoat separatist Lucien Bouchard in his Cabinet. With a high proportion of Quebec nationalists in Cabinet and in caucus he would not, he could not, speak out for Canada in Quebec. He was a hostage to his own party colleagues. This situation was not what Mulroney had intended. As he concluded after nearly two complete terms in office: "There are enough reasons for Canadians to be legitimately disappointed in me as a political leader. I don't want them taking their disappointments out on Canada. If they want to take it out on Brian Mulroney, it's easy. You throw him out of office."

Constitutional reform has been a gold-mine for academics. Their voluminous studies on the topic tend to be structured on two premises. First, answers to constitutional problems are assumed to be either correct or incorrect. This assumption is founded on a belief that if appropriate institutional mechanisms could be found then problems due to ethnicity, language, region and the economy could be mitigated or extinguished. Second, there is a belief that questions of leadership, competence of politicians, public discontent and raw electoral concerns have less relevance than institutions and can reasonably be left out of considerations of constitutional reform. Formal-legal discussions tend to underestimate, for example, the fact that without trust and confidence in institutions and leaders no proposals will work — no matter how well they are researched, developed and put in place. We contend that an assessment of the leadership factor is vital in understanding Canada's current difficulties.

QUEBEC AND MEECH LAKE

When the federal government went ahead with patriation of the Constitution without the approval of the separatist Quebec legislature in 1982, there was no significant outcry from Quebeckers. However, Quebec needed some compensation and was promised by Trudeau that it would have it. The Quebec Liberal Party, led by Robert Bourassa, concluded that the Constitution must be amended in at least five respects and ran his winning campaign in 1985 demanding the following concessions:

1. Quebec should be explicitly recognized as a distinct society within the Constitution.
2. Quebec should have a veto on future constitutional amendments in order not to be humiliated again.
3. Quebec should participate in appointing judges to the Supreme Court of Canada.
4. There should be limitations on federal government spending in provincial jurisdictions.
5. The immigration rules should be strengthened to give Quebec more constitutionalized authority in the field.

Since 1982 it had been generally agreed that the federal government would offer Quebec a new deal, a "renewed federalism" that would set the constitutional record straight. However, in 1984, before this was accomplished, Trudeau resigned and John Turner took over as Prime Minister. Turner immediately called an election and was severely trounced. Following that 1984 election, the new Prime Minister, Brian Mulroney, undertook to respond to these Quebec demands. The story of how the federal proposals were formulated, attracting public antipathy for federal government arrogance and incompetence, is well known. Even staunch supporters agree that the procedure was bungled beyond belief.

The Meech Lake accord was designed to get Quebec's signature on the Constitution. The euphemistic language and myth created around this event assured that all later discussions were based on what might, at best, be called a gross exaggeration. Canadians were told they had to "bring Quebec back into the constitutional family," "welcome Quebec back aboard," and make offers and concessions to "bring it back into the Constitution." This was all nonsense. Quebec had never "left" Canada or been "out" of the Constitution. Since it was never "out," it could not possibly "come in" again, except of course in a symbolic, rhetorical way.

The emotionally charged language allowed Quebec to play the role of the aggrieved partner that had been bullied and humiliated by English-speaking Canada. This, too, was nonsense. Trudeau, who was responsible for the patriation scenario, was a French-Canadian from Quebec, and his Liberal governments had had consistent massive support from Quebec since 1968. In 1982, when the Constitution was patriated, 74 of 75 MPs from Quebec were Liberals, and a third of the Cabinet was from Quebec. The Quebec provincial government, which was a separatist government at that time, did not sign the Constitution (although Lévesque had agreed to drop Quebec's constitutional veto during the discussions), but it was certainly not the case that French-Canadians from Quebec had no role in the patriation agreement. However, this myth — for obvious partisan reasons — was stated and repeated *ad nauseam* by the Conservative government until everybody believed it.

Prime Minister Mulroney's approach to acquiring the missing signature was to create a large package with bits and pieces and goodies to entice all the signatories. It was intended to be the highlight of Mulroney's career as Prime Minister. The government proposed the Meech Lake accord, an agreement to amend the Constitution along the lines suggested by the government of Quebec, and offered a political side deal for premiers who wished to reform the Senate.

Prime Minister Mulroney followed the unfortunate precedent set by Pierre Trudeau in 1982. He abandoned the successful, historically proven method of constitutional reform in this country which was to proceed on an issue by issue basis, solving one problem at a time. That earlier approach allowed serious reflection on the need for change and made it clear what consequences would be brought about by the revisions. The package deal allowed Trudeau to get enough support to patriate the Constitution, but he did not anticipate the severe problems that would arise for proceeding without Quebec's signature. He bargained hard for Canada, but he had not prepared the country for the weak leadership to follow. Under Mulroney the package-deal approach created constitutional overload. No one bargained for Canada.

Flaws in Process and Substance

The Meech Lake proposal was recklessly flawed, both in the process and substance of the agreement. There were two major problems with the process the Prime Minister chose. The first mistake was to adopt a rigid and polarized form of dialogue; the second was to establish a process of constitutional reform which was unclear, muddled and inconsistent.

The dialogue was stunted by a government that negotiated, in private, a document that had to be approved as it was presented with no changes possible. Public discussion was further narrowed by the promotion of a "two-vision" concept of Canadian federalism. On one hand there was said to be the vision of former Prime Minister Pierre Trudeau, based on a strong, bilingual federal government. On the other hand was the vision of Prime Minister Brian Mulroney of a decentralized federation of strong provinces working with the federal government. There were, our leaders told us, no other options or compromises.

This simplistic form of dialogue spawned and exacerbated the constitutional crisis. It was a "frontier approach" to constitution building in which there are only good guys and bad guys. Constitutional reform is infinitely more complex than this black and white juxtaposition allowed. Yet Sheriff Mulroney encouraged the dichotomy. Canadians had to be for or against the accord in its entirety — accept either the Meech Lake accord and the Mulroney vision, or reject it and accept Trudeau's.

Canadians who wanted to embrace Quebec but saw grave dangers in the Meech Lake accord were frustrated by the lack of options open to them. There are not just "two visions" of Canada; there may, more likely, be 26 million visions. But the Meech Lake accord contained proposals that required the unanimous consent of the provinces and the federal Parliament by the end of June 1990. Quebec wanted the accord intact as it had been negotiated, but responsible critics in many other provinces found serious problems that they wanted fixed before it was signed. According to the Constitution, this had to be done within a three-year time limit or the accord would disappear into oblivion. The stage was thus set for a dramatic confrontation between French and English Canadians.

The second major strategic flaw in the Meech Lake process was its authoritarian nature. In theory, there are three basic processes by which to achieve constitutional reform. The most democratic is to let the people decide through an election or referendum. The most authoritarian is to let top political leaders decide on their own. The third is Canada's actual constitutional process which allows the federal Parliament and the ten provincial legislatures to decide without consulting the people.

Stuck with this third process, the federal government and some provinces found it difficult to restrain themselves from crying foul and bullying those legislatures which honestly rejected the Meech Lake proposal. This turned the constitutional process into a *pro forma* farce.

The Conservative architects of the constitutional accord managed to delude themselves and some others into thinking that Canadians had to accept Meech Lake with its flaws or Canada would disintegrate. That was nonsense. Rather than a take-it-or-be-doomed accord, a flexible constitutional proposal should have been put to Canadians for debate. The process the government adopted gave only two rigid options. Quebec had to have the flawed accord or lose face; the rest of the country had to submit or put the country at risk.

If an election had been called over Meech Lake the government would amost certainly have been voted down. The Mulroney government chose the most authoritarian process possible. The eleven top leaders decided on an unamendable package full of fuzzy, ambiguous concepts and tried to impose it on their legislatures. This meant that rational discussion was stifled at the outset. And, when the topic could have been aired in the 1988 election campaign, it was overshadowed by the free trade issue and hardly mentioned by political parties anxious to avoid the fallout.

Canadians did not want to choose between the simplified "two visions" of Canada, nor did they approve of the less than democratic process that was foisted on them. They did not want eleven first ministers closeted late at night like poker players making secret bargains and deciding the future of Canada; they wanted to understand the implications of the constitutional changes and to have a say in them.

Besides this dogmatic and confrontational process, the Meech Lake accord was also flawed in its substance. The proposals included Quebec's five demands but they were badly written, vague, and included several woolly concepts meant to be swallowed wool and all. Moreover, the proposals were so extensive that they had to be passed by two different types of amending formulae. Some issues required the rule of two-thirds of the provinces and 50% of the population while others required the unanimous agreement of all the provinces.

The Meech Lake proposals would have decentralized the country through several major changes to the Constitution. Of the various amendments, three were particularly worrying to federalists. First, the Constitution was to be interpreted in a manner "consistent with the recognition that Quebec constitutes, within Canada, a distinct society." Quebec was constitutionally mandated "to preserve and promote this distinct identity." The concept of distinct society was undefined in the agreement so that dangerous possibilities were inherent in it. The Supreme Court could have agreed with a Quebec grab at power using this clause. Or, on the other hand, if the Supreme Court ruled that Quebec went too far in some project then Quebec nationalists could have claimed that the court had acted for Canada and against Quebec. There was no way Canada could win.

Second, the accord would have reduced the federal government's ability to use its "money power" to initiate a national program, such as a national child-care policy, in areas of provincial jurisdiction. And third, a veto would have been given to every province over future constitutional amendments — making it extremely difficult to change the Constitution in the future and thus further reducing federal government power.

In its desire to get an agreement at any cost the federal government was negligent in clarifying its proposals. The federal opposition parties were afraid to dissent, presumably for fear of losing votes in Quebec.

In the final analysis, the Meech Lake accord was defeated because it required unanimity from the provinces, and two provinces (Manitoba and Newfoundland) failed to pass the necessary resolution before the ratification deadline of June 23, 1990.

When the proposals did not obtain unanimity, the whole package was dead and matters became even more complicated. But Canada did not expire with Meech Lake as the Prime Minister had threatened. Life went on. However, the Quebec independence issue — dormant since the 1980 referendum — was given a new burst of respectability. Predictably, Premier Bourassa announced he would not attend any future federal-provincial conferences, and the Quebec National Assembly passed Bill 150 which required a referendum on "sovereignty" to be put to the people by October 26, 1992.

For over two years Canadians debated the pros and cons of the Meech Lake accord. But it was the wrong debate. The question should not have been "Meech Lake or no Meech Lake?" but "What is the best constitutional arrangement for Canada?"

A NEW CONSTITUTIONAL APPROACH

Following the death of Meech, there was an appropriate period of political mourning followed by numerous government-sponsored wakes and memorial services in the form of conferences, symposiums, federal-provincial meetings and even a Royal Commission about what to do next. Having insisted that it was Meech or death, Prime Minister Mulroney needed time to resuscitate the corpse.

The public was satiated with constitutional bickering, but still it went on, as groups prepared their demands for the next round of bargaining. Americans were mystified by the political anthropophagi taking place above their northern border. A joke circulated that two prisoners, a Canadian and an American, were each given a last wish before their execution. When the Canadian prisoner asked if he could please debate the Constitution just one last time, the American rolled his eyes and said, "Then just shoot me dead right now."

Unfortunately, the government ignored the report of the Charest Parliamentary committee which had provided detailed proposals to amend the Meech Lake accord but left its substance intact. That sober report had received all party agreement in the House of Commons, but it was left shelved and forgotten. Instead, another new strategy was devised which created a handful of new constitutional packages even larger and more indigestible than Meech.

Kill Them With Kindness

In a June, 1990 confidential briefing to *The Globe and Mail*, Prime Minister Mulroney made some candid remarks which revealed what his new constitutional strategy would be. He indicated that he would delay and temporize until all the political forces could come to some agreement. He would kill his opponents with kindness. "Anything that happens ... is going to be killed with kindness in the future. You will not be able to get me to ever cut off debate on a constitutional resolution. They can go on for as long as they want — years. I want to hear everybody, I want them recorded. I want them filmed. I want documents. I want... and if I've missed anybody I'm going to reopen it.

"And then when it's done, then we are going to take it and we're going to pass it. Which means that other people are going to have to do the work and they'll be — the country will be better off, the process will be better off, the politicians will have a lot less say in it, which is what should happen and it'll be better for Canada because it will be close to the people."

Following this strategy, the Prime Minister responded to the wave of populism in the country by raising more democratic procedures — some new, some old. Constitutional reform had become the most important single issue of his years in office, and it is on this issue that he will be judged as a Prime Minister and leader of Canada. The succession of tragi-comic events will be engraved in history. The highlights are worth remembering.

In order to quell the populist element, the Prime Minister and his new constitutional minister, Joe Clark (who better to kill with kindness?), initiated new consultations with the people and the premiers, minus the Premier of Quebec who boycotted all meetings. The earlier harder-line strategy which was based on a set of perceived principles about how a decentralized federation should operate was given over to an absolute brokerage model of negotiation.

The Spicer Royal Commission

The first concrete step in "killing with kindness" was the Spicer Royal Commission. Headed by the former official language commissioner Keith Spicer, its mandate was to consult the public about grievances and wishes for new constitutional proposals and clarify the very idea of Canada. And of course it was meant to keep the public occupied while the government pulled itself together and prepared a new proposal to replace Meech Lake.

On the positive side, the Commission provided a forum for some anxious and concerned Canadians to express themselves. But by the time the report was completed on June 27, 1991, the commissioners had been infected with the "Canadian Malaise" epidemic and were almost as divided and quarrelsome as the people they had interviewed. The Commission's mandate had been to listen and to educate. It did listen. At least four hundred thousand Canadians vented their frustration and gave their views of what is wrong with their country. Whether many were educated in the process is questionable.

Since the critics were self-selected rather than chosen by a proper sampling technique, there was no way of knowing how representative their disgruntled views were of Canadians as a whole.

One could only surmise from comparison with more scientific opinion polls the extent to which these "straw poll" complaints were shared across the country.

The litany of complaints brought out at the Spicer forum was no surprise. If there was a Canadian alive who was unaware of the public's unhappiness with politicians in general and Prime Minister Mulroney in particular, that was remedied. The report did, however, help to clarify some perceived problems. And since one must be clear about a diagnosis before offering a prescription, that was helpful. But just what was the cause of the illness and what political prescription would remedy it?

Unfortunately, the Spicer report was unable to sustain a logical connection between the complaint and its cure. It provided no clearly defined idea of what Canada is or could be, and no coherent suggestions about how to actualize Canadian aspirations. For example, the report upheld a vision of a united Canada which respects diversity. But then it recommended taking government funding away from multicultural groups, an action which would increase recrimination and charges of favoritism.

The report found that Canadians were worried and unhappy about the country's economic direction. Consequently it recommended that the government clarify why traditional values needed to be usurped by market forces. Again the commissioners badly missed the point. Too many Canadians were, and are, unemployed, too many business have gone under, too many cuts have been made in transportation. Health care is in jeopardy. Policies that have traditionally held this country together are being eroded. No government information program is going to make Canadians feel better about market forces that cause hardship. Only changing the economic direction of the country will. And the present government supports the harsh realism of laissez-faire capitalism regardless of its human costs.

The report did address some of the country's major fault lines. It said that many Canadians are upset with bilingualism as a national policy. It recommended an independent review of the official language policy and how it is applied. But since the Commissioner of Official Languages already issues a report every year which is discussed in Parliament and examined in minute detail, this proposal was not particularly helpful. Native Canadians, too, received respectful recognition by the comissioners, with a recommendation in favour of native self-government and recognition in the Constitution.

After great expense and enormous publicity, the Spicer Commission report fizzled like a defective fire cracker. The public had had its say and the report is now stored on shelves alongside thousands of other government documents.

The Last, the Almost Last and the Next Proposals

The stage was set for a new government initiative. The Prime Minister introduced his new constitutional package known as *Shaping Canada's Future Together* on September 24, 1991. This time the proposals were *not* supposed to be engraved in stone; comments and proposed changes were encouraged. For a while, there was little reaction as Canadians of all political persuasions were nervous about being depicted as naysayers, or worse yet, against Canada if they attacked the proposals. Much of the commentary centred on the good intentions of the government rather than on the contents of the package itself.

The government promised to mend its ways and listen to the people, and even offered a definition of "distinct society," a term which had been kept ambiguous the first time round. However, apart from that one definition, practically everything else cried out for precision and explanation. There were hundreds of concrete amendments hidden in the garb of 27 global suggestions. Not only were the proposals themselves vague, but the result of the relations among them was completely unknown, possibly even unknowable.

Once again, the proposals were too decentralizing and too multi-layered to allow effective and efficient government. Again they created the possibility of a checkerboard Canada. About the only proposal missing to decentralize the country was to move the capital from Ottawa to Moose Jaw. A few examples make this clear.

The residual clause — peace, order and good government — which has been used in the past to give necessary powers to the federal government was to be weakened by giving "non-national matters" to the provincial authorities. This indicated that the environment, for example, might be construed as a provincial matter so that federal regulations would not apply.

The "declaratory power" which was used to allow the federal government to take control of grain elevators and keep its transportation moving during the Depression was to be eliminated. The West had supported the decision to use such power during that period, but later they worried that Ottawa might use the same power to control oil wells during the energy crisis of the 1970s. Should the federal government give away powers which might be needed in an emergency? It would be unwise, given that no one can safely prejudge the future needs of this country.

Besides giving up such precise powers, the government proposed to withdraw from several specific jurisdictions. Some withdrawals were reasonable, such as in job training, but proposals to "streamline" other powers were more controversial. Surely there is a major role for the federal government in areas such as wildlife conservation and soil and water conservation where "streamlining" was also proposed; such environmental concerns do tend to spill over provincial borders.

Another major area of concern arose over the reform proposals which would have created a complicated morass of federal institutions. The Senate, as proposed, was too powerful compared to the House of Commons as a policy and law-making body — giving it the right, for example, to ratify major order-in-council positions, a right which is denied to the House of Commons.

The document also committed the government to give MPs "more free votes and to reduce the application of votes of confidence." This was mere rhetoric. The government had made this same recommendation in the mid 1980s but never acted on it. The government can already "free" its backbenchers at any time, on any vote, but it does not do so because cohesive political parties are, and should remain, an integral part of Canada's form of government. At any rate, the motivations and behaviour of future MPs cannot be significantly directed by the Constitution.

The *pièce de résistance* in the proposal was a new layer of appointed government — the Council of the Federation — to be added on top of the House of Commons, the newly elected, more powerful Senate and First Ministers' conferences. This undemocratic body, consisting of 13 representatives — one appointed by Ottawa, one by each of the provinces and territories — would have had a major impact on shared-cost programs, ratified the federal government's new economic powers and set up guidelines for raising and spending taxes. Such a council would have been in constant conflict with the elected Parliament of Canada over these important tasks.

Instead of streamlining government and making it more efficient and less expensive, the document actually proposed to create a cumbersome monster of institutions with the potential to generate more problems than it could solve.

Dobbie-Beaudoin and the Five Constitutional Conferences

The federal constitutional suggestions in *Shaping Canada's Future Together* were examined at length by a Joint House and Senate Committee on a Renewed Canada (known as Dobbie-Beaudoin) in order to produce yet another set of proposals. The government's 27 proposals were mildly criticized by the committee and savagely attacked in Quebec. The Dobbie-Beaudoin committee itself became the object of debate and derision for its poor organization. When Carleton university students interviewed members of the committee, they discovered that many of the politicians did not understand the details of the present constitution, let alone the implications of *Shaping Canada's Future Together*.

In keeping with its promise to allow public input, the joint House and Senate committee held five constitutional conferences across the country. However, there was no deeply hidden consensus about Canadian political arrangements waiting to be plumbed by public meetings, merely a confused and discordant babel of social, economic and language interests. In fact, in the conferences, efforts were made to add even more controversial proposals to the constitutional deliberations, such as ensuring that half of all Senators would be women, entrenching agriculture protection for western farmers, and guaranteeing price protection for Prince Edward Island potatoes.

No one was surprised that the conferences did not produce a consensus. The process was just more of the Mulroney strategy to "kill with kindness" and wear down the opposition to his decentralizing proposals.

The few participants who attended the conferences emerged with glowing reports about how much they had learned about other Canadians and about the system of government and its problems. They felt renewed in their commitment to the country, and projected the image of veritable love-ins. But since it was impossible to provide such an intensive learning situation and camp-like experience for every Canadian it was, from an overall perspective, a waste of time and money.

Since neither the government nor its proxy organizations could choose individuals who represented Canadian viewpoints and attitudes in a fair way, the conference views were unavoidably unrepresentative. Charges of manipulation and improper choice of delegates haunted the conferences from beginning to end. No proper, scientific sample of participants representing the universe of opinions could be called together in just five conferences. Public opinion polls would have been a better method for ascertaining the overall Canadian interest. In fact, the government already posessed such polls, but refused to make them public.

After these extensive hearings, the joint committee presented a revised set of proposals on February 28, 1992. The Quebec reaction was to remain aloof and distainful. Neither the government's *Shaping Canada's Future Together* nor the Dobbie-Beaudoin proposals were formally offered to Quebec and the other provinces, but they were turned down in principle by members of Quebec's political elite as insufficient to provide the type of framework required to keep Canada together.

As for the Official Opposition, the federal Liberals, they had issued their own nine-point agenda on constitutional reform in April 1991, but by July 1992 their leader, Jean Chrétien, was sufficiently disillusioned to suggest that a moratorium on constitutional reform should be considered.

The Constitutional Circus Marches On

Despite all these reports and public consultations the federal government still had no acceptable proposals. And instead of collapsing with exhaustion from all the kindness, public cynicism and criticism of the whole process was growing. Since Quebec in effect vetoed *Shaping Canada's Future Together* and the Dobbie-Beaudoin committee report, the federal government was forced back to the drawing board yet again.

The Prime Minister put the next phase of constitutional meetings in the hands of his flexible and popular deputy, Joe Clark. Under Clark's guidance the federal government called several meetings with nine provinces, two territorial governments and four aboriginal groups. The aboriginal groups themselves then enlisted economic, women's and nationalist umbrella groups to advise them. Quebec did not attend. The first of these meetings to draft new constitutional proposals to offer to Quebec took place on March 12, 1992. Four months later, on July 7, 1992 an agreement was reached by these leaders in what they termed the "Pearson agreement" (Mike Pearson would most certainly not have approved the decentralizing deal, but the agreement was reached in the Pearson building so that name stuck).

Meanwhile, Back in Quebec...

The Meech Lake failure did not kill Canada, but it did mark the end of a united Conservative Party. After the accord died on June 23, 1990, Mulroney's hand-picked former separatist leader, Lucien Bouchard, left Mulroney's Cabinet and formed the Bloc Québécois, a small band of dissident Quebec nationalists who already held seats in the House of Commons. Many of the remaining Quebec MPs were uneasy and had to be courted.

The Quebec government, meanwhile, continued to be bound by Bill 150 which called for a provincial referendum on sovereignty by October 27, 1992. The National Assembly set up the Commission on the Political and Constitutional Future of Quebec (known as Campeau-Bélanger), hearings which led to provincial consultations and, eventually, two parliamentary committees — one to examine the costs of sovereignty and the other to examine any offers on renewed federalism that might come from Canada.

Quebec's most divisive input into the constitutional debate came on January 28, 1991 from the Liberal Party's Allaire report, *A Quebec Free to Choose*, which proposed drastic decentralization of the country. Quebec would "exercise exclusive discretionary and total authority in most fields of activity." According to the report, 22 domains should be in the exclusive power of Quebec, including

communications, energy, industry and commerce, regional development and income security. Ottawa was assigned only currency,
customs and tariffs, debt management and transfer payments. Decisions of Quebec courts on these jurisdictions and other questions
would no longer be appealable to the Supreme Court of Canada.

The strong decentralizing thrust of the Allaire report was totally
unacceptable to most Canadians because it would have weakened the
country. However, it was intended to keep pressure on the federal
government and set a strong negotiation position for Quebec, and that
it accomplished.

The Allaire proposals cried out for asymmetry with different
status for different provinces or regions within the country depending
on their special needs. Canada already has some asymmetry now, for
example in the fields of agriculture, immigration and the environment. But this does not mean that further asymmetry would be good
for the country. If asymmetry is to apply in a comprehensive manner,
Canadians should insist on three general rules:
1. It should not confer *unique* benefits on one province that are not
   available to others; if there is to be asymmetry it should be
   "asymmetry without privilege."
2. It should not provide an economic advantage to one province over
   another.
3. It should assure that rights to government services, and obligations
   to collaborate and pay for them, are parallel.

Clearly, these rules would not be acceptable to the sponsors of
the Allaire report. Nor would Allaire asymmetry be acceptable to
provinces outside of Quebec without clarification and agreement on
these or similar principles.

THE PEARSON (BUILDING) PROPOSALS

By the spring of 1992 it was time for Mr. Mulroney to begin a new
count-down. The federal government and the provinces were under

pressure from Quebec's looming referendum which was set to take place by October 26, 1992. On July 7, the federal government (led by Mr. Clark), nine provinces, the two territorial governments and native leaders came to a tentative agreement. The agreement represented, to a large extent, what the major provincial players bargained for — a Triple-E Senate for the West, self-government for native peoples, a veto and "distinct society" recognition for Quebec. In total the proposals would have engendered a massive decentralization to the provinces and a drastic weakening of federal authority. Quebec representatives had neither attended the meetings nor accepted the agreement it produced.

The list of proposals was cobbled together out of fear and hope. Desperate to get a deal, Joe Clark adopted them without enunciating a single new principle of his own about how the country should be governed. Once more, the proposals contained an extensive devolution of powers which would have weakened the federal government's ability to make economic and social policy. That was not, of course, the official view.

Characterized by those present at that decisive meeting in the Lester B. Pearson building as a "constitutional breakthrough," the proposals would have amended the Constitution in multiple respects. The thrust of the deal can be described simply. Quebec was to get everything mentioned in the Meech Lake accord, including a veto over future constitutional amendments, in return for satisfying Alberta's desire for a Triple-E Senate (which westerners said was required because of the way they had been treated by the federal National Energy Program). Aboriginals, too, were to have their wishes granted.

Once again, the process entailed considerable flailing about by the parties concerned, giving the impression that no one was in charge or knew where negotiations were headed. There was further evidence that the federal government was more concerned with getting a deal than with achieving arrangements which would actually make a workable constitution. From a journalist's perspective this did not seem to matter. News commentary tended to concentrate on whether the agreement would "fly" with all the provinces and "sell" in Quebec. An "agreement at any price" was necessary to save Canada. The do or die atmosphere was shades of Meech all over again. Clark did not seem to be concerned that Canadians would have to live with the agreement a long time — considering that important amendments would have required provincial unanimity in the future.

Once again, the sad truth is that no one stood up for Canada in the negotiations. Joe Clark's assignment appears to have been to get an agreement at any price. As far as the public knows he never once told the premiers, "No, the federal government won't go along with this or that proposal because it would be bad for Canada as a whole." As Mr. Clark himself pontificated: "I can't recall another time literally since Confederation where there has been so much agreement on such a wide range of issues." It is not hard to get an agreement if everybody gets what they ask for, Mr. Clark. But what will happen when Canada has no more to give?

THE CHARLOTTETOWN ACCORD

The Pearson agreement drew Bourassa out of his bunker in Quebec City. After two years of boycotting constitutional discussions, he returned to the bargaining table on August 4, 1992 along with the Prime Minister, the other premiers and the leaders of the territories and the aboriginal communities. The result was a complex and highly controversial constitutional deal known as the Charlottetown accord, agreed to on August 28, 1992. It consisted of an agreement on principles — not a legal text — about what changes should be made to the Constitution, further political accords to be negotiated, and an agreement to put the tentative principles to the Canadian people in a country-wide referendum.

Despite the fact that they were unanimously approved, the Charlottetown proposals are dangerous. To show the potential damage they could inflict on Canada we shall examine the basic proposals in the *Consensus Report on the Constitution* separately.

Meech Plus or Minus

The Meech Lake proposals had consisted essentially of five parts — distinct society, a veto, immigration powers, restrictions on federal spending and appointments to the Supreme Court, each of which responded to a demand by the government of Quebec. The same demands were addressed by the Charlottetown accord, but it went much further. It included proposals to add a new clause to the Constitution which would ensure that "Quebec constitutes within Canada a distinct society, which includes a French-speaking majority, a unique culture and a civil law tradition." As well, the role of the legislature and Government of Quebec "to preserve and promote the distinct society of Quebec" was affirmed.

In other areas, such as immigration, the Charlottetown proposals slightly softened Meech Lake. Under Meech, Quebec was to obtain a fixed share of immigrants to Canada. Under Charlottetown, Ottawa would only be committed to negotiate agreements with the provinces, a policy which is already the practice. And, if the federal government spends money in a new Canada-wide shared-cost program in a field of exclusive provincial jurisdiction, as in Meech, a province would be able to claim compensation if it had a program which was "compatible with the national objectives." On Supreme Court appointments, there is no change from Meech. The current practice of appointing three Supreme Court judges from Quebec would be constitutionalized, only new Ottawa would be required to select judges from lists supplied by the provinces.

The main difference between Meech Lake and the Charlottetown proposals is over the constitutional veto. Charlottetown would give all provinces a veto over future constitutional changes to the country's major political institutions. On the surface this looks as though it meets Quebec's earlier demands, but in fact it falls far short. The veto would apply only "after" the Charlottetown changes were made part of the Constitution, in particular those concerning reform of the federal institutions. As in Meech, Quebec wanted the veto to ensure that it could prevent a Senate reform of which it did not approve. Quebec also wanted a veto over the creation of new provinces, but the Charlottetown accord would allow the federal Parliament to create new provinces through a simple bilateral agreement with Ottawa. Moreover, since the proposed changes to the amending formula would increase the number of matters that require unanimity, every province — not just Quebec — would have an even greater capacity to veto further constitutional proposals. If this change is accepted, it will be almost impossible to correct any deficiencies in the Constitution at a later time.

Clearly, most of the "offers" that were made to Quebec in Meech Lake were included in Charlottetown, but some were damped down. The deal, therefore, is bound to find opposition both inside and outside Quebec.

The Canada Clause

The Charlottetown deal calls for a major innovation in the way we govern Canada. A "Canada Clause" is to be included in the Constitution to express fundamental Canadian values. That clause is extremely important as it will be justiciable — that is, the courts will be able to use the Canada Clause to guide *all* future interpretations of the *entire* Constitution. As an interpretative provision it will be binding on the courts in every constitutional case.

Eight "fundamental values" are expressed in the Canada Clause. They include values related to democracy, aboriginal rights, the distinct society of Quebec, linguistic duality, racial and ethnic equality, individual and collective human rights, the equality of female and male persons and the equality of the provinces.

At first glance, this appears to be a sensitive statement of the collective goals of a diverse and caring society. But, on careful scrutiny, the Canada Clause proves to be replete with errors of consistency and fairness.

The Canada Clause proposed a hierarchy in fundamental Canadian values. While *Canadians and their governments* are committed to the development of language minority communities, only *Canadians* are committed to racial and ethnic equality, individual and collective human rights, the equality of female and male persons and the equality of the provinces. The implication is clear. Governments are committed to take action — and presumably to spend money — to defend some groups but not others.

Moreover, some Canadian groups are left out of the Canada Clause altogether. Whereas the *Charter of Rights and Freedoms* stipulates equality for people who are physically or mentally handicapped, and asserts that individuals should not be discriminated against by age, the proposed Canada Clause overlooks these values altogether. Thus, the clause provides a hierarchy in which some groups are protected by government, other groups are protected only by Canadians, and still other groups such as the handicapped, seniors, and children are not mentioned at all.

Division of Powers

The new proposals call for the decentralization of some current federal authority. Job training and culture are to be given to the provinces congruent with their present authority in the field of education. The Charlottetown accord is nuanced on these two topics, however. In job training, the federal government's power would be narrowed to exclusive jurisdiction for unemployment insurance and involvement in the establishment of national objectives for labour market development. As well, the federal government would be excluded from a meaningful role in retaining workers for the new global economy. Culture, too, would be artificially divided between two levels of government. The provinces would have exclusive jurisdiction over culture "within the provinces," and the federal government would retain powers over existing national cultural institutions, including the grants and contributions delivered by those institutions. If these proposals are constitutionalized, the designation of "culture" as an area of exclusive provincial jurisdiction will lead to endless constitutional wrangling in the Supreme Court.

As well, the Charlottetown accord calls for the federal government to withdraw from several areas including forestry, mining, housing, recreation, tourism, and municipal and urban affairs. Some of these are very significant for the future of Canada and others are less so.

Take the example of housing. Will the constitutional proposals alter existing housing policy? Maybe yes, maybe no. The federal government now supplies approximately 1.8 billion dollars in funds for old social housing and approximately 100 million dollars for new social housing annually. Nowhere in the proposals is it indicated whether or not appropriate funding will be transferred to the provinces to maintain services at their present level. This incomplete proposal only calls for more deals to be made on the subject.

Given the federal Conservative government's track record for cutting back on other public services, there are grounds to believe that there may be some fudging going on here and that the details of funding were not mentioned for a very good reason. If the provinces are left to find the money, they will not be able to. They, and not the federal government, will end up being blamed for the cuts.

At best, in all of these decentralizing proposals, policies on which Canadians have grown to depend might remain intact. At worst, some important policies, such as subsidized housing for the needy, might be discontinued. This rather wide spectrum of possibility proves that the federal government still does not have a handle on viable constitutional change.

Native Self-Government

The demands of native peoples were not addressed by the Meech Lake proposal and, in the final analysis, this omission contributed to its demise. Native MPP Elijah Harper was the key figure in the Manitoba legislature's rejection of that accord. His dramatic action made him a folk hero and stimulated increased pressure for native self-government in the next round of constitutional negotiations.

In one early demand the leader of the Assembly of First Nations, Ovide Mercredi, asked for equal status for all 54 aboriginal languages with English and French and for all aboriginal groups to have equal political status with the provinces. In May, 1992, Joe Clark announced in Vancouver that all provinces except Quebec had accepted the "third level of government" principle for native peoples. Clark said that the details of how such a third level would relate to existing federal and provincial jurisdictions would have to be negotiated politically rather than entrenched in the Constitution.

The Charlottetown proposal goes a long way toward satisfying aboriginal demands. The Canada Clause says that aboriginals "have the right to promote their languages, cultures and traditions and to ensure the integrity of their societies, and that their governments constitute one of three orders of government in Canada." The proposals also include an expanded definition of aboriginal people, a political accord for the Métis, and treaty rights to be affirmed in the Constitution. During the first five years of this agreement native groups would not be able to employ these clauses in cases before the courts.

Even among staunch supporters of the aboriginal cause, there is, and will continue to be, considerable controversy over these undefined rights. Newfoundland Premier Clyde Wells worried out loud about whether the same of different laws would apply to native and non-native Newfoundlanders. The most direct attack on the concept of aboriginal rights came from a Quebec government report entitled "An Analysis of the Impact of the Constitutional Recognition of the Inherent Right to Self-Government." It described the proposal as "unquestionably the most profound change to the political structure of Canada since 1867."

The report declared that a self-government clause would "threaten Quebec's territorial integrity and weaken provincial powers," and without Quebec's approval would probably be unconstitutional "because creating a new order of government requires the unanimous consent of all the partners to Confederation." Further, it argued that such an agreement would violate the *Charter* which calls for all Canadians to be treated equally under the law. It judged that approval of aboriginal self-government would be exorbitantly expensive, and that territorial disputes and land claims would have a much stronger legal basis. As the report put it: "There is reason to believe that the aboriginal peoples will not be satisfied with the lands they now occupy; they will seek to acquire new land." Brian Craik, Director of Federal Relations for the Grand Council of Crees of Quebec, replied that Quebec has nothing to fear, that in time the Crees will claim vast areas of northern Quebec and the Mohawks huge parts of southern Quebec, but only as a "starting point for a workable solution for all parties involved."

Elsewhere, the main complaint was that too many small governments might emerge if native self-government were placed in the Constitution. Worries were also expressed that band and tribal councils would want to negotiate their own laws to govern schools, justice systems, child-welfare agencies, and other community organizations. Critics asked if self-government could mean up to 600 tiny governments. If so, would this constitute a new form of segregation? Would the Criminal Code apply to native peoples? Would educational standards, or environmental regulations, apply?

Advocates say there is no worry on either theoretical or practical grounds. The Charlottetown deal insists that a law passed by a government of Aboriginal Peoples "may not be inconsistent with those laws which are essential to the preservation of peace, order and good government in Canada." But this does not eliminate the fear, because the text also specifies that "this agreement would not extend the legislative authority of Parliament or the legislatures of the provinces." The practical aspects of native self-government are clearer. The process would be extremely drawn out and there are only about 30 aboriginal governments which could be created in the next half a dozen years. The proposals also circumscribe the power of aboriginal groups to act precipitously by calling for an orderly transition negotiated "in good faith." Moreover, some provinces may still be able to opt out of the agreement, and there is no guarantee how much federal or provincial funding will be available to pay for self-government.

Even among those who favour self-government for native peoples, there is a concern that the participants in the negotiations did not fully understand the implications for such issues as jurisdictions, lands, resources, human rights and economic and financial considerations. The Charlottetown accord is replete with ambiguities and contradictions. Should constitutional amendments of such magnitude be left to the courts to rule on after five years elapse? One wonders if the self-government clause is a "blank cheque," and why it is necessary to make such massive changes in such a short time. As Ed Roberts, a Newfoundland minister, put it when he described the first aboriginal package as an "incredible mess": "We are doing things and we know not what we do. I don't say that with any joy or any happiness, but believe me we have not thought them through."

Social and Economic Union

According to the Charlottetown agreement the country should enjoy a social and economic union. It sets out objectives for the social union on such topics as providing "a health care system which is comprehensive, universal, portable, public administered and accessible," "high quality primary and secondary education to all individuals resident in Canada" and "reasonable access to post-secondary education." Laudable as these goals are, they are reminiscent of the Constitution of the former communist USSR — they are merely slogans and platitudes. Even the Canadian first ministers realized this when they concluded in the agreement that citizens could not rely on these statements in the courts. They are — as they agreed — "not justiciable." Honest politicians would also have pointed out that a non-enforceable social charter is no substitute for real parliamentary capacity to set national standards.

The Charlottetown agreement also commits governments to free trade within Canada. Among other clauses it calls for "the free movement of persons, goods, services and capital," "full employment," and a "reasonable standard of living." Again, this is ridiculous. These clauses (which are to be placed in the Constitution) cannot be taken before the courts. We are being asked to trust our political leaders' rhetoric about our aspirations. Even Michael Wilson, the government's trade minister, attacked the Pearson proposals as providing too many exceptions — enough to outweigh any good done by the provision of an economic union. Jeffrey Simpson of *The Globe and Mail* called it an "emasculated" common market clause. The final Charlottetown agreement is even worse than Wilson and Simpson imagined. It does not *commit* the eleven governments to anything at all; nor does it allow the courts to make decisions on the basis of the economic union clause. It is plain hogwash.

Proposed Institutional Changes

The Charlottetown proposals call for a drastic and foolish overhaul of the federal institutions. The changes can be summarized briefly as follows:

Senate

a) The Senate is to be elected either by the population of a province or territory or by a legislative assembly.

b) The Senate is initially to total 62 Senators. It will be composed of six Senators from each province and one Senator from each territory.

c) The Senate will not be able to force the resignation of a government.

d) The Senate will have some authority over legislation:

i) It will be able to delay revenue and expenditure bills for 30 days by a suspensive veto. After that period, the House of Commons will be able to act on its own. But fundamental policy changes to the tax system (such as the Goods and Services Tax and the National Energy Program) are to be excluded from this section and handled as ordinary legislation.

ii) It will have veto power over all legislation on natural resources.

iii) It will be able, by a majority vote, to trigger a joint sitting with the House of Commons on all ordinary legislation. The joint sitting would have ultimate authority over this referred legislation.

iv) On matters which materially affect the French language or culture a double majority of anglophone and francophone Senators would be required.

e) The Senate would have to ratify the appointment of the Governor of the Bank of Canada and other key federal appointments.

House of Commons

According to the Charlottetown proposal, the membership of the House of Commons will be increased to 337. Ontario and Quebec will obtain 18 additional seats, BC four additional seats, and Alberta two additional seats. As well, Quebec will be guaranteed no fewer than 25 percent of the seats in the House of Commons. The issue of female and aboriginal representation has been left for future consideration.

Federal Government

The Charlottetown accord would also repeal the federal power of reservation and disallowance of provincial legislation. The federal "declaratory power," which permits the government to declare a "work" for the general advance of Canada and bring it under the legislative jurisdiction of Parliament, would also be amended to ensure that it can only be applied to new works or rescinded with respect to past declarations with the explicit consent of the province(s) in which the work is situated.

Institutional Madness

The proposed Charlottetown amendments to our government institutions are much worse than "not perfect." They will only perform efficiently and effectively when Canada has perfect politicians and perfect parties — and how often is that?

The proposed rubik's cube of institutions will work effectively *only* when the following *two conditions* prevail.

First, we will need a majority, not a minority, government. Since the Second World War, almost half of our governments have been in a minority situation. And the strong presence of the Reform Party and the Bloc Québécois suggests that we will have a minority government after the next general election.

Second, there will have to be a federalist government in Quebec. Has everyone forgotten Premier René Lévesque? There is a reasonable probability that the separatist Parti Québécois will win a provincial election again — and soon.

Without these two conditions in place the constitutional arrangements will further weaken government and fracture the federal system. If there is a separatist government in Quebec, the federal government will be handicapped in dealing with it. The current constitutional arrangements are much preferable.

The truth may be inconvenient, but the flaws in the deal must be addressed. The sooner the better. Let us count ten major ways the proposed institutional arrangements are inadequate.

One: It will increasingly be regarded as unfair to give Quebec 25% of the seats in the House of Commons in perpetuity. Today Quebec has 25.3% of the population. Demographers predict it will drop below 25% by the end of the decade and down to 23.5% by the year 2011. By contrast Ontario, British Columbia and Alberta will all grow substantially.

Two: Equal provincial representation in the Senate will be an increasing source of irritation. Ontario, with a population of 10 million, gets six Senators, the same number as Prince Edward Island which is the size of Nepean, a suburb of Ottawa. The distortion is too great.

Three: National standards should be maintained in federal institutions. With these new proposals we will have Senatorial elections in some places and nominations in others. It is not an improvement to allow the Quebec National Assembly rather than the federal Prime Ministers to appoint Senators. In the United States, Senators were first appointed by the states. That procedure proved so corrupt that they changed to elections. Are we so backward that we want to revert to government appointments to the upper house?

Four: Since there are to be simultaneous elections for the House and Senate, appointed Senators from Quebec make no sense. After a general election which sweeps one party into power in Ottawa we could have the Quebec National Assembly appointing Senators who do not reflect that change. The electoral results would count every place but Quebec. How naive can we be?

Five: There will be too many ways for the Senate to tie up the government and prevent it from acting. Fifty percent of the Senate (representing at minimum only 13.2% of the Canadian population) will be able to block all taxation on natural resources and force all ordinary legislation to a joint sitting with the House of Commons.

Six: The Senate's power to send all ordinary legislation, including such major issues as the Goods and Services Tax, to a joint sitting with the House is dangerous. Government business will be disrupted and responsible government will be diminished. The Senate will be toothless — like a blackfly!

Seven: The double majority of anglophone and francophone Senators required to pass language and cultural legislation could prove troublesome. A double majority means that as few as three Parti Québécois Senators (there likely will only be six francophones) would be able to block all the remaining Senators from action. And, a majority of English Senators could block something Quebec wanted in this field.

Eight: The Senate is to have a controlling veto over higher government appointments. The House of Commons, the major democratic institution, will be able only to scrutinize appointments. Why? So that a tiny proportion of the public representing the smallest five provinces can prevent appointments which the government, a majority of the members of the House of Commons and most of the people want?

Nine: If the Senate delays the legislation of a minority government, the situation will be destabilizing for responsible government. When there is a divided House, the joint sitting would not be controlled by MPs. The combination of House and Senate could block legislation and force the formation of a new government, a new cabinet coalition or a general election. As well, politicians often block one bill in order to prevent a totally different one from getting through. Senators will be able to block appointments, taxation on resources and language and culture bills and force ordinary legislation to a joint sitting until they get compromises on other matters of which they disapprove.

Ten: The costs of Parliament will be much too high given the size of the Canadian population. Taxpayers will pick up extensive new bills. A House of Commons with 337 seats will make it more than three-quarters the size of the United States House of Representatives (435) with one-tenth the population.

The costs of paying for the new Parliament will be great. Members cost more than Senators and elected Senators will cost more than appointed Senators.

Is this going to help decrease the deficit and national debt? Bob Rae says premiers will now be able to talk about the economy. But first they will have to find several million more dollars to pay for the former Senators, new Senators and the extra 42 MPs — and their pensions!

The Charlottetown Senate: A Dangerous Attraction

Prime Minister Mulroney was cornered by the proponents of a Triple-E Senate. His 1984 and 1988 electoral successes and the composition of his cabinet and caucus today are based on a Quebec-Alberta alliance. If he opted for what Quebec wanted — namely Meech Plus — he lost support in the West, particularly in Alberta, unless he also bought off westerners with a form of Triple-E. For that reason, he accepted the Charlottetown proposals for the Senate — a combination of deals and counter-deals that would make Hudini wince.

Mulroney was correct to prevent the adoption of a full Triple-E Senate as was advocated particularly by Don Getty, Gary Filmon and Clyde Wells. Triple-E is not the answer to regional discontent. In fact, it would prove to be a serious threat to equal rights, responsible government and legislative efficiency in Canada.

However, Mulroney was wrong to accept even the equality provisions of the Triple-E concept as he did in the Charlottetown accord. There is no escaping the basic fact that the most democratic form of representation is one person one vote — "rep by pop." That kind of basic equality was the goal of our forebears and should remain so. Ideally, all citizens should have the same amount of political weight, no matter who they are, where they live, or how they vote.

Distorting this basic democratic principle to provide extra representation for less populous regions or special groups is no more worthy a goal than to provide extra representation for the rich. Regional aspirations should be met, but establishing a basically unjust system of representation is not the way to do it.

The best way to protect regional aspirations is to elect strong voices to the House of Commons and insist that they are well represented on the front bench of the government. Unfortunately, under the Charlottetown provisions the representation of the more powerful provinces will grow at the expense of the weaker provinces, and Quebec will be given 25% of the seats in perpetuity.

Supporters of Triple-E point to the examples of Australia and the United States to illustrate what a good idea it is. They are using rose-coloured glasses that filter out some very harsh realities.

Take the United States comparison. The Canadian and American political systems are very different, and no single feature which is transferred form one to the other will work the same way in its new surroundings. In particular, the American system has a strong President whose powers can be used to overcome the divisions caused by a deadlock between the House and Senate.

This is simply not the case in Canada. We do not have a President to promote unity for the country and effectiveness for government. Deadlock and delay would paralyze government in this country if Senate powers were equal to those of the House. How could a do-nothing government solve regional alienation?

Even assuming the best, which would be that a US style Senate could work as well in Canada as it does in the United States, there still would be no justification for adopting it. There is no reliable evidence that the United States' political system delivers peace, order or good government any better than the Canadian system we already possess. Quite the contrary.

Australia, Triple-E supporters argue, may be an even better model than the United States for Canada to follow, because it has a relatively similar system of government. This is true. But even here one should be extremely cautious. The reality is that Triple-E down-under has done little to ameliorate regional tensions and has some-times made matters worse.

The problem with simple comparison is that one must look beyond the similar formal-legal structure of Australian government to the politics within it. For example, Australian politics is organized by parties, and party discipline in the upper chamber ensures that Senators only rarely vote against measures supported by their own party in the lower chamber. In effect, this means that Australian Senators are *not* more effective advocates for the regions they repre-sent than the members of the lower house.

The Australian Senate can also become a house of obstruction. During the mid 1970s, an intractable deadlock between the Senate and the House of Representatives over the budget precipitated disso-lution of both houses and a constitutional crisis. The political process has since returned to "normal," but the possibility of another such crisis remains and is worrisome to Australian experts. Under the Charlottetown proposals, such deadlocks would develop regularly between the House and Senate.

Canada and Australia both have responsible government in which the majority party dominates. Citizens know who to credit or blame for different policies and outcomes, and ideally can support the incumbent party or choose among other competing visions or platforms at election time. In Australia, responsible government is preserved at the expense of regional representation. When the pro-posed new Canadian Senate blocks legislation what happens to the idea of responsible government?

How will the government be held responsible to the people when the proposals it initiates are ultimately turned down by the Senate? Clearly, the two concepts of responsible government and regional representation are in irremediable conflict. If we decide regional representation should dominate, then we have to jettison responsible government, separate the executive and legislative branches, and adopt the ramshackle American congressional system and possibly elect a President.

Advocates of Triple-E would lure Canadians from the relative safety of the frying pan into the fire. Grievances must be addressed. But we must not delude ourselves into believing that *all* complaints west of Kenora are worthy of redress, any more than are the myriad of daily woes from Ontarians, Québécois and Maritimers.

Regional discontent is a serious problem. Canadians must decide how best to provide an institutional voice for diverse agendas and aspirations without pandering to fear and selfishness. We need strong leadership on this question in order to find compromises which will best serve Canadians as a whole. Once again, someone should stand up for Canada and against ill-conceived regional proposals.

Suspending "representation by population" and replacing it by "representation by province" constitutes a vicious attack on liberal democracy in Canada. The idea that an individual's vote is worth more or less depending on where he or she lives invites short-term hostility and long-term deadlocked governments.

The situation is complicated further by new actors on the political stage, including native, women's and other interest groups. They all want their own hand-chosen members in the Senate. We need institutions which aggregate, not divide interests, so that governments can respond to the collective needs of the country.

The main problem with the existing Senate is that it lacks legitimacy because it is based on political appointments. The Charlottetown agreement pretends to remedy this. In fact, it makes it worse. The Senate will consist of a hodge-podge of elected and appointed members because the rules can be different for each province. Quebec, for example, will be able to appoint its six Senators by a vote in the National Assembly. Ordinary people will not even have to be consulted. Such a Senate will have no more legitimacy than the current upper house. At the federal level all positions should be filled by elections which follow the same rules.

HOW WILL HISTORY RATE
PRIME MINISTER BRIAN MULRONEY?

Brian Mulroney's place in history will be decided by the outcome of the constitutional negotiations: the October 26, 1992 referendum and the formal changes to the Constitution. He is responsible for escalating the emotion around the issue and reviving separatism in Quebec. He is responsible for the bungled strategy and content of the Meech Lake and Charlottetown accords. The interview in which he bragged about how well he had handled the Meech agreement — it just needed "a roll of the dice" — justifiably won him the wrath of the Canadian electorate. Constitutional reform is not a crapshoot.

The constitutional process remains a mess. with the Charlottetown accord, Brian Mulroney again employed the bargaining techniques he had learned as a neophyte lawyer: a combination of negotiation by exhaustion and the idea that if you give up too much in one negotiation you can recoup it later. That tactic may work in business-labour relations, but it is a short-sighted and destructive strategy for achieving something as vital and permanent as a constitution.

Whatever proposals are finally accepted to cure Canada's constitutional ills, they must work in time of crisis, not just in good times. The best way to ensure this is to make changes in only very small, explicit steps. The Charlottetown agreement has many evident flaws. And, because of its complexity, we should expect it to give rise to many more problems that are not yet apparent. It presents serious dangers for the country. Many clauses are undefined, contradictory, complicated, and not properly spelled out. They contain hidden mines that will explode only after they are in place.

The whole Charlottetown package should be shelved or voted down until a new general election gives Brian Mulroney, or some other leader, a mandate to negotiate another deal. Without a general election, the government should have proceeded one small constitutional step at a time. No proposal should have been accepted unless it could be demonstrated satisfactorily that it would provide Canada with a Constitution that would make it a more prosperous, just, or free country than it already is. It is a tall order, but it is the minimum we should accept. There is no rush. A country which ranks first on the UN's Human Resources Index can afford to take its time and think changes through carefully.

If, by chance, luck, or the guidance of angels, the Charlottetown accord is accepted and actually *works,* many of Brian Mulroney's past errors will be forgiven. Few of us believe in magic, fewer still believe in a politician's conversion on the road to an election. There is no doubt that the Prime Minister wants a *perceived* constitutional success — one which would give him a window to quit or run again. If he is successful, he will run in the next general election. If not, he may yet stand up for Canada by standing down before the next general election.

The Charlottetown agreement on which the Prime Minister has staked his career is replete with institutional flaws and dangers for Canada. It would reduce the central government to a hollow core that is powerless to act in the interests of all Canadians. Because of this, Brian Mulroney may well go down as the worst Prime Minister in Canadian history.

6 The Political Challengers: Friends And Enemies

"... there was the awakening instinct of a nation in search of its soul, a nation perhaps a little wiser than some of its leaders."

— Rudyard Kipling, "Canada's Path to Nationhood" Speech delivered to the Canadian Club of Ottawa, October 21, 1907.

It would be lazy and inaccurate to claim that all politicians are the same, that seekers and holders of public office are equally self-interested or visionary, careful or corrupt. They are quite definitely not all the same. Some are Canada's friends and some are its enemies.

We may love our enemies and wish for their redemption, but enemies they remain. Their artifices should be rejected and their schemes defeated, lest we allow our enemies to overwhelm what is good in us and tear down what we have built.

Our friends, being mortal, have many faults, but a friend at least is one who seeks to help, not hinder. A friend's advice may be wisdom or folly, but never would it be a secret plan to divide and ruin.

The duty of each responsible Canadian is to caution and criticize the friends of this land and to expose the country's enemies. In the current time of overlapping problems and dangers, it is clearer than ever who are the builders and who the destroyers. We have looked at

Brian Mulroney's leadership qualities. Let us now turn our gaze to some other men and women who are helping to shape this country's destiny.

FRIENDS OF CANADA

Jean Chrétien: A "Little Guy" in the Shoes of a Giant

"Nobody picks no fights in Canada,
Not with nobody they ain't met;
Nobody starts no wars in Canada,
Folks tend to work for what they get;

Take me under that big blue sky
Where the deer and the black bear play;
May not be heaven, but heaven knows we try
Wish I was in Canada today."

— from Billy Bishop Goes to War
by John Gray with Eric Peterson

Jean Chrétien is by far the most experienced federal political leader. During some twenty-five years in the House of Commons, he has held no fewer than ten cabinet portfolios, spearheaded the "Non" campaign during the 1980 Quebec referendum, and was Minister of Justice overseeing the patriation of the Constitution. The other party leaders are raw amateurs by comparison. Audrey McLaughlin, leader of the New Democrats, did not see the inside of the federal legislature until 1987 and has never sat on the government side. Bloc Québécois leader Lucien Bouchard came to Ottawa as a Progressive Conservative in a 1988 by-election. He spent nearly two years on Mulroney's team before defecting in the spring of 1990. The Reform Party chief Preston Manning, whose father was the premier of Alberta, has never held public office.

When Mr. Chrétien returned to the House of Commons in 1990, he did not run in Quebec but in the New Brunswick riding of

Beausejour. This was widely (and correctly) interpreted as a sign of weakness, though it made good political sense. It would have been foolhardy for any non-separatist to campaign in a province stinging from the recent death of the Meech Lake accord. Since his election, the Liberal leader has been a good deal less popular in Quebec than his party, which seemed the only real rival for the Bloc Québécois.

Since before he won the leadership of his party in 1990, Chrétien has been dogged by often mean-spirited attacks by the media. The artless epithet "yesterday's man" has been repeated so often in the press and on the airwaves that no doubt some people have come to accept its accuracy. Completely absent from the comprehension of some of Chrétien's critics is the fact that, occasionally, ideas persist over time because they are good ideas. If Chrétien's views on Confederation are similar to those of Trudeau, it is because Trudeau possessed an enduring vision of Canadian unity. Like his predecessors, Trudeau understood the necessity of a strong central government able to speak for all Canadians, for universal programs of health care and social assistance, and for the state to intervene from time to time in the economy and society for the public good.

The logical alternative to "yesterday's man" would be "today's man" — or, as some would have it, the political "flavour of the month." The advent of urban invertebrates who bend to every whim of every provincial or special interest group is not surprising today. Rather, it is the result one should expect when those who possess coherent principles are routinely vilified as insufficiently reflective of today's biases and trends.

Chrétien's leadership style is in flux. The tough "little guy from Shawinigan" image may not sell in the '90s, when Canadians seem to want glossy pseudo-leaders who will do what they are told and not make tough decisions. He has lost his appeal in Quebec and the western provinces. In some part, family and health problems may be to blame for the fact that Chrétien has not again sparkled as he did during the 1984 leadership contest. He was impatient to get the job but has been remarkably quiet since achieving it. His best hope is that the electors will come to realize he is one of the few leaders who never strayed from strong support for the *Charter of Rights and Freedoms* and an effective federal government. Until the 1992 Charlottetown accord, Jean Chrétien stood up for Canada against those who would tear it apart. However, in approving this document he has gone the way of his predecessor John Turner and bowed to pressure which would strip Parliament of its ability to set national objectives and enforce national standards.

Until he half-heartedly threw his weight behind the August 1992 constitutional proposals, Chrétien's vision of a united Canada was admirably consistent. The passionately pro-Canada message he brought Quebec during the referendum campaign in 1980 sold to a majority then but might convince only a minority today. Trudeau did not deliver on the renewed federalism he had promised Quebeckers. The so-called "rejection" of Quebec has become a permanent, if misleading, part of the political lore of that province, and this legacy remains with Chrétien, depressing his popularity in Quebec. It also explains why so little is known of his character and vision.

Despite his sincerity and his firm opposition to the advocates of division, Chrétien has not performed nearly as well as he should have as leader of Canada's traditional governing party. He has often temporized — or is it dithered — on matters of fundamental consequence. There is some dispute about whether Chrétien has been "handled" too much by his "handlers." Indeed, it seems out of character for the "petit gars" to sit on the fence, even though this inaction has kept his party well ahead in the polls.

When the rest of the country had gone on to discuss the Pearson proposals, Chrétien called for the Prime Minister to follow the recommendations of the Dobbie-Beaudoin commission. He advocated a referendum without due consideration for its possible consequences. His nine points on the Constitution were unnecessarily vague, and there was some question about whether he had been co-opted by Mulroney, or vice versa. When the August 1992 constitutional agreement was produced, it met most of Chrétien's nine, vague points for a renewed federal system. Recognizing that Canadians were fed up with constitutional wrangling, Chrétien would have preferred a 10-year moratorium. Instead, he was bested politically by Mulroney. He caved in, accepted the deal and joined the "yes" forces in the referendum. It was a political response rather than one "straight from the heart." He was not strong enough to stand up to the blackmail, carve out an alternative constitutional agenda and demand what was best for the country. During the next election the Liberal leader will be forced to stake out his position more clearly on the question of national unity and explain to the people why he is still Canada's best chance at the federal level.

An important part of what makes Chrétien a friend of Canada rather than an enemy, and distinguishes him from the legions that follow the ideology of difference, is his understanding of the role of leaders. Angry with political poltroons like Alberta premier Don Getty or Quebec opposition leader Jacques Parizeau, Chrétien exclaims that the "duty of political leaders is to appeal to what is best in people, not to pander to some people's worst instincts for cheap political points." The Liberal leader recognizes that Canada is wounded by the deliberate exacerbation of regional and ethnic cleavages by self-interested politicians. As one American political leader put it, one can neither add by subtracting nor multiply by dividing.

The Liberal leader recognizes the obvious affinity between the secessionist Bloc Québécois and its English Canadian equivalent, the Reform Party. Both new sectional parties play on the public's cynicism with politicians and institutions, and so contribute to the worsening of Canada's problems. Preying on the fears of citizens pummelled by the recession, and counting on latent racism, these parties jointly are the antithesis of Chrétien's view of Canada: "Preston Manning is the flip side of Lucien Bouchard. One wants a Canada without Quebec; the other wants a Quebec without Canada.

The way Preston Manning can succeed is if Lucien Bouchard succeeds — and vice versa. They need each other. But Canada doesn't need either of them."

Chrétien draws scowls and predictable separatist vituperation when he demands that the enemies of Canadian federalism provide reliable evidence to support their position. The Liberal chief insists the onus is on secessionists to demonstrate how the social and moral, cultural and economic well-being of Quebeckers would be enhanced by independence. Chrétien calls on the moaners and beguilers of the separatist camp to "prove that independence or sovereignty will be superior to federalism in promoting values such as generosity, tolerance, social justice, cultural diversity, the rights of individuals and minorities."

In a similar vein, Chrétien mocks the narrow views of Preston Manning and the Reform Party, especially the fallacious assumption that equal treatment of citizens means the *same* treatment: "In Preston's world, if you support the idea of a multicultural Canada, too bad. You can no longer count on multicultural programs to battle racism or to promote tolerance. Tolerance is not a priority for the Reform Party. If you have been disadvantaged because of your race, colour, religion, sex or age — or because you have a disability — too bad. In Preston's world, you can no longer count on the government to provide equality of opportunity for all citizens. The Reform Party does not believe in those kinds of programs. They want to get rid of them."

The Liberal leader decries the leadership of accountancy offered by those who emphasize fiscal and trade arrangements within Confederation to the exclusion of all else. To speak only of the purely economic opportunities and benefits of Canada, while ignoring the liberty, tolerance, and rich diversity that characterize life north of forty-nine, is in Chrétien's view to "cheat Quebeckers of their birthright" as Canadians. The Liberal leader reminds us that the Quebec of which all Canadians may rightly be proud did not develop in a vacuum, but within the context of Canadian federalism.

An essential component of Chrétien's vision of Canada is the redistribution of wealth between persons and provinces, such that some measure of equality of opportunity may be known from sea to sea. The system of equalization payments is in his view "proof of the generosity of all Canadians toward each other, wherever they live in Canada." This opinion is not shared by organizations such as the Canada West Foundation, which employs curious accounting techniques to declare a $100 billion loss for Alberta from equalization and energy pricing. In a sense, Chrétien is attacking the neo-conservative organizing ideology of the western world, because such programs consciously defy the principle of "every man for himself."

Similarly "liberal" is Chrétien's opinion of government administered universal health care. This national treasure, guaranteed by the Trudeau-era *Canada Health Act*, is currently under examination by free enterprise Americans who desire to deliver health services and insurance for a smaller portion of the gross national product than at present. Chrétien observes that medicare is "a hidden asset that not only makes Canadian society more human and caring — but could give us a major competitive advantage over other nations." The answer to rising costs is not, in his opinion, to abandon the principles upon which the health insurance system was founded, namely universality, portability, comprehensiveness and public administration.

Liberal Party support for a national referendum on the Constitution was not new. When Chrétien was Minister of Justice in 1981, the government proposed to place provisions for a referendum as part of the amendment process in the new Constitution. This was in keeping with Trudeau's advancement of popular sovereignty over governmental sovereignty — vesting final political authority in the people, not in provincial or federal institutions. "Let the people say yes to Canada in a national referendum as soon as possible," said Chrétien, "then we can really start putting Canada back to work

187

again." This proposal, divisive as it is, indicates Chrétien's naive belief in the good judgment of the people.

Chrétien has long been a passionate defender of bilingualism as a defining and unifying phenomenon for Canada. As one smart aleck puts it, Chrétien himself is truly bilingual: he speaks broken English and broken French. The Liberal leader responds firmly to the shallow and ignorant attacks on bilingualism launched by the Reform Party and nakedly racist groups such as the Confederation of Regions (COR) party and the Alliance for the Preservation of English in Canada (APEC): "Official bilingualism does not force anyone to speak another language. It gives Canadians the right to deal with — and receive services from — their federal government in the official language of their choice."

Chrétien also defends bilingualism against detractors among Quebec francophones — the linguistic community it was intended most urgently to protect. Under the glare of the largely nationalist Bélanger-Campeau commission in Quebec, Chrétien argued that, "without a doubt, Canadian bilingualism — that is, equality of status of both languages — promotes the status of all francophones in Canada, regardless of where they live, their income or their social standing." It is worth remembering that Chrétien was the only national leader willing to risk his political skin and stand up for Canada at that commission, which was set up shortly after the demise of the Meech Lake accord. His philosophy, which he fully understands will never be popular with French or English extremists, is one of a welcoming community, not an exclusionary club: "I am proud to be in a country where English is not restricted to the other nine provinces. There are a lot of people in my province of Quebec who are as much Quebeckers as any of us and who are English speaking and deserve to be protected like anybody else. That is a fundamental cornerstone of what we call Canada. "

Audrey McLaughlin: Leadership by Committee?

"If democracy is right, women should have it. If it isn't men shouldn't."

— *May Clendenan, Grain Grower's Guide,*
February 24, 1915

Leadership in the New Democratic Party of Canada operates according to a somewhat different principle from that of the other parties. Namely, the party is supposed to set policy and the leader is supposed to be bound by it, rather than the other way around. That is not to say the NDP leader has no influence in the setting of policy, but her role is more circumscribed than that of Reform leader Manning and is dramatically less powerful than that of Mulroney or Chrétien.

At the same time, Audrey McLaughlin employs a leadership style that is unique among the major party leaders. Her propensity to delegate authority is not new, but her consensual approach to problem-solving distinguishes her leadership technique from that of her rivals. Some observers have gone so far as to suggest, perhaps not totally without foundation, that this constitutes a "feminine" style of politics hitherto unknown at the national level in Canada. More to the point, McLaughlin appears to employ a decision-making mode that is atypical in her chosen field of endeavour.

McLaughlin acknowledges that "being a member of a majority in our society who are, traditionally, a powerless group has a tremendous effect on the way I look at social relationships and power relationships." Her background in social work and social policy gives her additional understanding of the travails of poor and struggling Canadians and those who, without support, would be pushed to the margins of the community.

More important than her style is McLaughlin's image. In choosing their leader in the winter of 1989, New Democrats appear to have identified four characteristics in Audrey McLaughlin that they saw as particularly appealing. First, she is a woman. Gender is not a valid

189

reason for choosing a leader, and the NDP has been alternately praised and scorned for selecting the "amazingly unamazing" McLaughlin primarily on this basis. Then again, if a person in a historically disadvantaged group is never given a special boost, there is little chance for that person to rise through a system founded and maintained by relatively advantaged persons. Ms. McLaughlin has more than gender to offer her party and her country, but there is good reason to believe many New Democrat delegates thought it was about time for their party to have a female leader.

The second image question, and one which is not really a corollary of the first, is that she is a feminist. Given the considerable linkages between the NDP and certain sections of the women's movement, and mindful of the strides that party has made toward numerical gender equality among delegates, candidates and officials, the ascent of a feminist to the highest post was probably inevitable. Certainly, it makes sense for Canada's social democratic party to have a leader who is advertised as carrying the torch for a generation of women seeking empowerment. Her life story is presented as an inspirational tale of independence in the face of adversity. McLaughlin has had children and career, and when she split with her husband, she packed a pickup truck and headed for Klondike Country. This is a much more interesting and circuitous route than the usual one which takes aspiring politicians from private tutors through law school to the legislature.

A third characteristic is her position on native rights. A strong supporter of aboriginal self-government, McLaughlin has a good record on what is one of the most controversial issues of the day. Fourth, and least important of these characteristics, is the fact that she is from neither Quebec nor Ontario. A leader from the hinterland may be welcomed by those feeling alienation from the "politics as usual" at the centre. A tiny but telling example of McLaughlin's influence in Ottawa is the fact that her tripartite idiom "from sea to sea *to sea*" seems to have become a permanent part of Canadian political discourse.

It would be unkind to agree with the jokesters that NDP stands for "No Discernable Policy." There are days, however, when New Democrat policy contains more mystery than solution. At any given time, the NDP has at least two policies on Confederation, one of these voiced by the single member Quebec caucus, the "sovereignist" Phil Edmondston. The case of Edmondston, who won the Chambly by-election in 1990, is particularly instructive with respect to McLaughlin's leadership abilities. The difference between McLaughlin and Chrétien is clear — the Liberal leader would not tolerate an anti-federalist carrying the party colours. Even if a separatist were duly elected by a constituency association and by voters in an election, Chrétien would not permit a known separatist to sit in his caucus. The Liberal Party of Canada's national unity position may not be the hottest scheme in *la belle province*, but at least the Grits have only one policy on this topic.

Audrey McLaughlin's plan for Canadian reconciliation can be pieced together as follows. First must come a scheme of economic cooperation and mutual respect, whereby people are guaranteed the dignity of a job. McLaughlin does not believe it is acceptable for the industrial reserve army of unemployed people in Canada to number over a million. The country has, in her estimation, ample resources and expertise to eliminate poverty and to reduce dramatically the shock of layoffs or redundancies.

The new "economic charter" for Canada assumes a mixed economy of private, public and cooperative enterprise. McLaughlin avoids the usual NDP argument that the market should not be permitted to control certain social processes or the distribution of certain goods. Instead, she proffers the much more palatable rhetoric that the market should not be *forced* to undertake certain onerous tasks. The result is the same — state intervention in the contest of capital and labour — but the packaging is much less "socialist." This softer tone toward business may represent a departure from the NDP reputation as a party of grim faced "injustice-collectors," and create a threat to the Liberal and Conservative middle ground.

The second ingredient in McLaughlin's recipe for Canadian serenity is a social covenant affirming equality of condition as well as equality of opportunity, and of course such central social democratic planks as medicare, high quality and accessible education, and honourable retirement for elderly citizens. In her words, "a just country, a truly united country, has a social contract with its people based on compassion, cooperation, decency and equality."

Number three on the NDP agenda for future unity and prosperity is a recognition at the national level of the urgency of collaboration between all groups in society to preserve the natural environment. As any sane person knows, the survival of the human race depends on development that is sustainable, on production and consumption that is not poisonous to the earth. New for the NDP is the understanding that the preservation of jobs and the protection of the ecology are related; that no investment in the biosphere can happen if everyone is on the dole.

Fourth on McLaughlin's list is constitutional renewal, which must be brought about not merely with the consent, but with the involvement of the governed. The process of defining a new supreme law should be attended by extensive consultation with groups through their local or national organizations. Taking the ideology of difference to its logical conclusion, McLaughlin declares that "a new Constitution must include a stronger recognition of collective social, economic and environmental rights, a recognition that defines those rights and responsibilities and addresses the needs of communities." This smacks of the same "community of communities" nonsense that Joe Clark peddles, and for which he is rightly chastised. Absolutely the last thing Canada needs is more power or recognition for sub-cultures and special interests.

In addition to sacramentalizing sub-Canadian group identities, the NDP leader calls for greater provincial and territorial influence in national institutions such as the Bank of Canada and in the federal legislative system. Moreover, she hints at the imposition of quotas to ensure "more equitable representation" of natives, ethnic minorities, disabled persons, women and "ordinary Canadians" in the political process. This last spike of McLaughlin's constitutional railway is an important one, for it marks where her scheme goes completely off the rails.

Put bluntly, the NDP constitutional agenda is long on philosophy and short on substance. McLaughlin speaks of a federal government being able to act upon the national will. In spite of this, she advocates decentralization of powers and direct provincial involvement in the operation of the national system of lawmaking, regulation and administration.

When she had to take a stand on the August 28 constitutional deal, McLaughlin and her party, like Chrétien and the Liberals, succumbed to political pressures. Despite some misgivings over gender parity and further recognition of ethnic miniorities, the NDP federal council voted unanimously to endorse the deal. Party interests were put before Canada's interest.

Audrey McLaughlin is a loyal Canadian of whom her party may justifiably be proud. She is not, however, providing better than mediocre leadership on the question of constitutional design. The internal rules of the New Democratic Party seem to contribute to followership at the top, rather than leadership. The NDP is excessively responsive to special interest groups and provincial demands and seeks to entrench that relationship in the federal political process.

The party's comprehension of the political dynamics of Quebec is nil, even as it does backflips to accommodate secessionists. At the same time, the NDP may be said to be a *semi-national* party, unlike the Reform Party or Bloc Québécois, which are *sectional* parties. The NDP has little support in *la belle province*, but it runs candidates there and attempts to woo Quebec voters to its cause. Party workers look on helplessly as the NDP begins its inevitable descent back into third place in the polls, as voters anticipate an election coming soon. Audrey Mclaughlin is a friend of Canada because she sees this country as a unified whole, even though her specific plans for maintaining that unity are flawed.

ENEMIES OF CANADA

Preston Manning: Partition by Default

"Now I'm so happy, no sorrow in sight,
Praise the Lord, I saw the light."

— from I Saw the Light
an American revival hymn

By far the most interesting political leader in Canada is Preston Manning. Prairie populist and fiscal zealot, he leads a party renowned for speed of growth, efficiency of operation and narrowness of view. Manning reaps discontent and sows discord, creating and sustaining popular illusions about the simplicity of solving the nation's problems. To those of us who would defend a strong federal government and a united Canada, which includes Quebec and respects linguistic duality and multiculturalism, Preston Manning is a public enemy.

The leader of the Reform Party has emerged as a political force only recently, but his experience with the machinations of politics began early in his life. Preston is the son of Ernest Manning, who ruled Alberta as Social Credit premier from 1943 until 1968. The bootstrap conservatism and religious fundamentalism with which the younger Manning was raised are not unusual in Wild Rose Country, nor are they necessarily cause for alarm. Once described as a "Christian guerilla working in a corrupt, secular world," Preston Manning is a member of the First Alliance Church in Calgary, which embraces male domination of society and the strict and literal interpretation of the Bible. Naturally, there is nothing inherently wrong with people possessing such beliefs — indeed, one of the founding principles of Canadian society is tolerance for different creeds and ideals.

The core of Christianity is amity, forgiveness and care, despite one's opinion of a neighbour's failings. What must be watched carefully is how Manning proposes to translate his own particular version of Christian thought into public policy. It is highly unlikely that Manning will publicly advocate perpetual male supremacy. Yet he does oppose programs like affirmative action that are intended to ameliorate the conditions of discrimination and disadvantage felt by women and by minorities and handicapped persons. Meanwhile, Reform doctrine is rife with intimations that family violence should be a matter for families, not the police or courts.

Scornful of what he calls the "secular fundamentalism" of feminists and environmental activists, Manning presents himself as a beacon of principled, conservative stability in a sea of rampant special interests and weak-kneed brokerage politics. Manning may be a religious fundamentalist, but his sour, divisive and exclusionary tones are hardly those of an evangelist. Self-reliance and strength of purpose are positive characteristics only if they do not disguise self-interest and unwillingness to listen. Canada exists because of compromise. The position of Manning on compromise is eloquently explained by a worker at the Reform Party headquarters in Calgary: "To compromise is to be unmanly."

The problem with Preston Manning is not his strong conservative principles. On the contrary, it is a rare delight to encounter a politician who actually seems to stand for something. What Preston Manning does *not* stand for, sadly, is Canada. He seeks to be the voice of disenchanted English Canada, speaking *against* its arch-rival, French Canada. Manning is the consummate sectional party leader, seeking further to divide this house against itself until, inevitably, the union is shattered amid threats and acrimony.

What makes Manning dangerous for Canada is the popularity of his simplistic political message, his calm and businesslike manner, and his personal charm. His slight physical stature and bespectacled bookishness do create an aura of knowledge and power. There is no appearance of a threat from a "hidden agenda" which would be dictated in the event that Reform were to wield final legislative authority. Yet a danger to Canada stems from the agenda openly advocated by Reform — the small-minded attack on bilingualism, the dogmatic approach to federalism, the ill-informed coveting of American-style republican political institutions, the crude and selfish disregard for health care and social assistance plans, and the array of nostrums and maxims by which Reformers seek to deflect criticism of a reckless scheme to eliminate the federal budget deficit.

Manning has been known to use the vague modifier "affordable" when speaking about health care — surely, Manning would say, one could implement "affordable" user fees or "affordable" extra billing. A cynic would interpret this argument as just another conservative coded message, promising better times for the wealthy and fiscal responsibility for the poor. The Reform boss insists that social programs should be "sustainable." While this makes good common sense, it is also true that the most easily sustained program is one without a budget.

In fairness to Manning, the Reform plan to make 15% budget cuts in all federal departments and eliminate the deficit in seven years is not driven just by neo-conservative ideology. Canada faces terrible choices in the future as the federal debt approaches $450 billion and the prospect looms of caring for an ever larger elderly population. Medical costs, especially for drugs and chronic care, soar out of sight, while many high wage manufacturing jobs are lost forever. The people are weary of tax increases and seem less willing than ever to share what they have with the less fortunate.

The Reform Party is counting on dissatisfaction and deliberately contributes to disenchantment with national institutions. The worse things get, the better for Reform, which declares for itself a kind of right-wing infallibility. The elimination of equalization payments and the strangling of social programs only have currency for people who are not interested in helping out fellow citizens. Most Canadians are not so callous. In some respects, Manning is counting on the voters being so distracted by, and distraught with, their own personal problems that they will not carefully examine the bizarre and drastic Reform agenda for smashing the federal government and advancing the cause of victimized wealthy white anglophones.

Manning describes his vision of a "New Canada" as a "balanced" deal between provincial governments, where each person and province can expect equal treatment. The country Manning envisions should be remarkable for "...the viability of its economy, the conservation of its northern environment, the sustainability of its social services, respect for human freedoms and roots, and governments that live within their means. It should include a New Deal for aboriginals, a New Senate to address regional alienation, and a New Quebec."

It is neither a mistake nor a coincidence that "a New Quebec" is the last item on Manning's list, because it is quite the least important. The New Quebec would possess only the same rights and powers as other provinces and would behave like other provinces, as one of ten equal partners in Confederation. Preston Manning knows these terms will never be acceptable to Quebec. Canada would be partitioned by default.

Manning tackles the "*deux nations*" problem head on, damning the generations of leaders who were so foolish as to attempt to save the country as a united whole. He counsels that English and French heritage in Canada are worthy of preservation, but says such work should be carried out only by "individuals, families, organizations, and... provincial governments." Attempts by the federal government to do more than this, to "politicize and institutionalize and constitutionalize English-French relations on a national basis and as a *raison d'être* for the nation itself — have led again, as they have in the past, not to unity but to crisis."

The conception of Canada as a bargain or compact between French and English Canadians, says Manning, leads to a dead end. The permanent division into "camps" so engendered produces useless schemes and counter-schemes, and wastes the people's energy. "Every constitutional and language controversy for the last thirty years," argues the Reform leader, "has been a signpost that has been ignored on a road we should not have travelled."

Constitutional entrenchment of the idea of two founding races is, in Manning's analysis, just a device for breaking down unity in a country of diverse ethnic communities. He claims that this notion fails to meet the objective of John A. Macdonald (or Trudeau) to reduce conflict and calm the fears of francophones. To the contrary, the two founding races model "relegates to second-class status the twelve million Canadians (including aboriginals) who are of neither French nor English extraction. Better to look forward to a federation of equal citizens and provinces, progressive people say, than to look backward to a federation of founding races."

Despite his lack of concern over potential separation, Manning sees Quebec as the key to achieving the constitutional changes he desires. As the "only province that can crack the Constitution wide open," Quebec may provide an opportunity for Reform to undertake certain alterations of the supreme law that would not otherwise be possible. Of course, Manning's shopping list will be rather different from Quebec's. He is especially interested in avoiding any form of "asymmetrical federalism," which he believes would be "the first step toward sovereignty association."

The Reform leader has quipped that "there are really three types of politicians with respect to the Constitution: those that are for it, those that are against it, and those that have read it." Manning misses the point of this epigram. If politicians are ill-informed about the Constitution, imagine how little substantive knowledge the voters have. To the average Canadian, "Section 92(10)(c)" sounds more like "Star Trek" coordinates than it does the significant if rarely used "declaratory power." This is natural enough. Most people are more concerned about daily matters such as mortgages, groceries and the price of gasoline than they are about amending formulas or concurrent jurisdictions. Reform's continuing call for direct public involvement in the constitutional and legislative processes, and for recall of recalcitrant politicians, has more to do with stirring up crowds than with making good laws.

From time to time, Manning trumpets the need for less "top-down" and more "bottom-up" decision-making, empowering ordinary people at the expense of elites. In principle, this is not such a bad idea — the people (mostly men) at the top need to be shaken up once in a while. Despite this, much of the Reform platform resembles less the "common sense of the common people" and more the reckless "bottoms-up" decision-making of the beer hall. For every problem, Reform has a monosyllabic solution suitable for quick memorization and savage implementation. No equation is so complex that Reform cannot solve it with axe or bludgeon. RPC support flows from the same kind of uninformed passion that won Ronald Reagan the White House for eight years, and sundry Socreds and Tories the Alberta Legislative Assembly for generations.

After several days of sounding out his largely western grass-roots party members, Manning declared his opposition to the 1992 Charlottetown agreement and his support for the "no" side in the October 26, 1992 referendum. He and his party branded the deal as a sellout to Quebec. His negative assessments of the proposal were based largely on the guarantee of 25% of the seats in the House of Commons for Quebec, the loss of a full Triple-E Senate for the West and other Quebec or French-related concerns. As in his earlier support for a constituent assembly, the exercise represents a rather shameless attempt to foist the narrow, francophobic Reform outlook onto the majority of Canadians.

Perhaps the most telling statement that Manning has ever made is his demand that no Prime Minister born in Quebec should be permitted to negotiate the break-up of Canada. This is not just a contemptible notion, but it is especially divisive and panders to the basest fears in the population. Without question this viewpoint casts doubt and suspicion on everything else that passes his lips. It is astounding that an intelligent and seemingly astute individual could fail to appreciate the destructive and provocative nature of such a claim. His "New Canada" clearly does not include Quebec. Canadians know this.

Fortunately for Canada, the prospect of a Reform government in Ottawa is a silly hoax. The party holds only one elected seat in the whole country. Support for Reform in Ontario and Atlantic Canada was never much larger than the margin of error in any given poll, and it is declining. As of the fall of 1992 Reform trails the Liberals somewhat in popularity in two of the three prairie provinces and in British Columbia. The Reform Party of Canada, far from being the new voice of English Canadians, was and is basically the party of southern Alberta. There is, however, a reasonable chance that, even with its unilingual, right-wing agenda, it could obtain enough seats to drive Canada to a five-party Parliament, in which case it might — just might— hold the balance of power.

Lucien Bouchard: Partition by Deceit?

"Not believe in Santa Claus? You might as well not believe in fairies."

> — *Francis Pharcellus Church to "Virginia"*
> *in the New York Sun, September 21, 1897*

Lucien Bouchard was a federal Minister of the Crown before ever being elected to the House of Commons. This unusual affair had the separatist Bouchard sworn in as Secretary of State some seven weeks before he won the Lac-Saint-Jean by-election in June, 1988. He retained his seat in the November 1988 general election and was appointed Minister of the Environment and made caretaker of the promising "Green Plan." There was never any question but that this *beau risque* entailed Bouchard's deliberate and public support for Brian Mulroney and the Meech Lake accord. Bouchard's ascent to the House was not conditional on anything, as far as the electors were concerned: he was a minister in the federal Tory government.

In May of 1990, Lucien Bouchard felt slighted by Mulroney's handling of constitutional negotiations. His logical response was to quit Cabinet and the Progressive Conservative party. The man who had fought for "sovereignty-association" in 1980, then accepted Tory patronage and changed his tune to renewed federalism, maliciously switched back again at the worst possible time for Mulroney, his party boss and old friend. In his May, 1990 letter to the Prime Minister explaining his departure, Bouchard explained that the sentiments underlying the process of negotiation about the Meech Lake accord were false and misleading. Canada, wrote Bouchard, was not worth even attempting to save: "We must stop trying to fit Quebec into the mould of a province like the others. Beyond the legal arguments, there is one argument that is unanswerable: Quebecers do not accept this mould. Their very reality shatters it."

Upon the formal death of Meech in June of 1990, Bouchard moved to set up a legislative group in the House of Commons working for the death of Canada. A handful of MPs followed him, to create the Bloc Québécois. The purpose of the BQ as stated in their draft manifesto is simple:

> The Bloc Québécois' mission in Ottawa is solely to promote Quebec's profound and legitimate interests and aspirations. On the federal scene, this formation is the single voice of those who, beyond partisan political allegiance, want to make Quebec a sovereign, pluralistic state, open to the world. The Bloc Québécois pledges to work toward the achievement of this objective throughout the process leading to the national Assembly's official proclamation of Quebec's sovereignty.

After discharging this mission, the Bloc Québécois will have no more raison d'être.

Had Bouchard any principles, he would have resigned from the House of Commons, given that he hopes to tear apart the country for which it stands. That he remains a Member of Parliament is testament to his opportunism and his ability to rationalize any iniquity provided it serves an immediate political purpose. Members of the Bloc have proven sufficiently unprincipled to swear a false oath of allegiance to Her Majesty (or to let one stand), and are happy to draw salary, benefits and eventually pensions from a federal government to which they are disloyal. When this matter came up on a point of privilege in the autumn of 1990, the Speaker correctly ruled that "only the House can examine the conduct of its members and only the House can take action if it decides action is required." The House prudently chose to do nothing, as any censure of Bloc members would have created further uproar and division in the population.

The head of the Bloc practises a form of demagoguery which is hardly original. Bouchard is guilty of the manipulation and negative outlook that typify politics of the 1990s in industrialized western countries. As in America and English Canada the loathsome politics of victimhood has new currency in Quebec, where poverty, unemployment, economic stagnation and the weather are always somebody else's fault. It is very convenient not to have to rethink policies or make tough choices. In Bouchard's case, the federal system is to blame for all problems — especially those which coincidentally are endemic to all capitalist systems — so the solution is plain. Wreck Canada, and poor maltreated Quebec will be freed from its shackled and impoverished state.

Bouchard foresees a limit to the life-span of his group. If the secessionist party achieves its goal, it will dissolve. In his address to the founding convention of the Bloc Québécois, Bouchard explained that the success of the BQ "will be measured by the brevity of its existence."

The Bloc Québécois possesses the political sensitivity of a lynch mob, with no ideological coherence beyond the desire to secede. When challenged, Bloc members tend to rely on the repetition of tired slogans typical of the Reform Party and on unsubstantiated rhetoric such as equating Quebec Tories with "Nazi collaborators." The urbane and colourful Bouchard has cobbled together a small crew of Tory turncoats and Grit deserters, as well as one ex-communist who won a by-election under the Bloc banner. Truly, there is less here than meets the eye.

The source of Bloc support is precisely the same as for the Reform Party — uninformed passion. The Bloc knows that for all their common sense and common knowledge the common folk have no subtle understanding of legal language or the constitutional division of powers. It knows the people have neither the time nor the inclination to become economic or constitutional experts. For this reason, the Bloc appeals to bare emotion: anger, fear, ethnic pride and so on rather than logical or intricate arguments.

The "rights industry" that has emerged since the advent of the Canadian *Charter of Right and Freedoms* is symptomatic of the phenomenon that underlies much of the current problem. Legitimate demands for inclusion and individual equality have yielded progress and moderation, but also parochialism and selfishness. When the best way to win a political skirmish is to be perceived as a victim, there is no higher goal to achieve than victimhood. This dynamic is clearly at work in the whining of the Reform Party about everything from mounting tariffs to Mountie turbans, from oil taxation to metrication. And it is painfully evident in the unsophisticated rantings of the Bloc Québécois.

The Bloc does not have a platform because it does not have any coherent ideas. The answer to everything is sovereignty. Never mind the billions in federal government transfer and equalization payments that have buoyed the Quebec economy in recent years. Forget that Quebec culture is vibrant and thriving after one hundred fifty years of political union with Ontario and the other provinces. Pay no attention to the million francophones outside Quebec that would be sold down the river. Just close your eyes and vote for secession, then everything will suddenly be better. Remember, you're a victim.

It was insensitive and politically hazardous for ex-Rat Pack member John Nunziata to call Bouchard a "traitor to Canada." It was also quite correct. Strictly speaking, how could it not be correct to brand as a traitor a person who preaches secession — whose project is the destruction of Confederation?

Having a small handful of secessionists in the national Parliament is a disgrace for that institution, but it is hardly cause for panic. Lucien Bouchard, a man whose greatest political achievement was to stab an old friend in the back, has led a ragtag band of leavers and deceivers to a back corner of the House. The Bloc can yet do great damage to the prestige and legitimacy of the federal system, but only if millions of Quebeckers can be defrauded, cajoled or intimidated into supporting secession. Bloc support may be "soft," but a soft majority on just one election day could destroy this great country.

Lucien Bouchard is on the national stage, preaching the death of Canada, because the Right Honourable Martin Brian Mulroney put him there. "Je me souviens" is the correct motto for this moment — let us remember who was the first Prime Minister to invite an avowed separatist to join his Cabinet. And let history judge Mulroney accordingly.

Jacques Parizeau: By Any Other Name

"We're gonna leave the Dominion,
We're forming up our ranks;
We'll borrow the money from Ottawa
And it's gonna be in francs;
And everything's gonna be wonderful
In our private country
When we all live under
The dear old fleur-de-lis."

— from The FLQ March
by "The Brothers-in-Law"

In searching for Canada's enemies, one quickly comes across Jacques Parizeau, the leader of Quebec's main separatist force, the Parti Québécois. A key player in René Lévesque's first PQ government elected in 1976, Parizeau at one time or another held all the primary financial portfolios of the province before he resigned in 1984. His election as the replacement for failed leader Pierre-Marc Johnston in 1988 was regarded as a victory for the hard-line nationalists in the party and a return "from the dead" for separatism.

Much has changed for the PQ since the reappearance of Quebec Liberal Robert Bourassa as premier. Today, the new age separatists in the Parti Québécois are more in tune with the obfuscation and misdirection of modern Yankee politics than were the separatists of Lévesque's era. Witness how the likes of Parizeau have decided that the vague term "sovereignty" is much more palatable and user-friendly than the harsh and accurate term "separation." Sadly, some people are fooled by this window-dressing. Yet secession, partial or complete, by any other name remains secession.

Parizeau speaks about the virtual departure of Quebec from Canada, retaining defence cooperation, Canadian currency, influence in the central bank, and the Free Trade Agreement with the United States. All other sovereign powers would revert to the Assemblée Nationale in Quebec City. This would be achieved by the magic wand of a Quebec referendum and unilateral proclamations by the premier and a majority of MNAs.

The only piece that is missing from the puzzle is the fact that this arrangement does not exist outside the exaggerated fantasies of a few weak-minded separatists. It is quite inconceivable that the rest of Canada would ever agree to such terms, notwithstanding the ineptitude and incoherence of the current federal government. Not even Mulroney and our present invertebrate premiers would permit the red maple leaf to become a flag of convenience for the economic élite of a French republic in Quebec. It is hard to accept that an otherwise respected professor of economics and longtime political agitator such as Jacques Parizeau can exhibit such total incomprehension of the political dynamics of secession.

Parizeau's leadership is not without critics among those allegedly loyal to Quebec yet disloyal to Canada. The PQ leader has mistakenly admitted two things: first, that independence is less popular during times of economic uncertainty; and second, that he should not have said this in public. Parizeau's call to postpone any Quebec referendum on the Constitution for two years was transparently connected to the state of the economy and the timing of provincial and federal elections. He has generously offered to resign if his forces are again defeated in a Quebec referendum on sovereignity, while at the same time threatening to "boot the rear end of Quebeckers who can't speak English." If his leadership fails, it is not inconceivable that Parizeau would be replaced by a more "mediagenic" personality such as Lucien Bouchard.

A gleeful Jacques Parizeau launched the Parti Québécois attack on the Charlottetown proposal. He derided Premier Robert Bourassa for selling out the vision of Quebec as one of two founding nations, and claimed that the distinct society clause not only offers no new protection for Quebec but actually threatens the province's French language legislation. Casting his net as wide as possible to catch everyone who disliked the deal, he maliciously called on Jean Allaire (who, eighteen months earlier he had call "insignificant, ridiculous and stupid") and other disgruntled Liberals to join his "no" forces in the referendum. The constitutional proposals, he said, were "unacceptable and dangerous" for Quebec. His party's strategy to defeat them is to "dump on" them rather than to sell sovereignty.

It is considered politically incorrect these days to draw attention to the dreadful consequences if Quebec separation ever becomes a reality. Imagine how ordinary Canadians would react if secession ceased to be an annoying threat and actually came about. Think about what would happen if the average Canadian should be confronted with the declaration, "tomorrow at noon, the country you grew up in, that nurtured you and to which you owe gentle allegiance, will exist no more." The immediate effect would be the radicalization of otherwise moderate people in English Canada, who would no doubt show uncharacteristic spite and cheerfully divert their trade to America or abroad rather than support secessionists. One hopes the treatment of francophones outside Quebec would be better than that of Turks in Germany or Muslims in Bosnia, but such hope might be vain. And what of the English speaking minority in west Montreal? What of the (mostly anglophone) natives in James Bay or Kanesetake? More than angry words would fly. The air would be filled not just with bricks and bottles, but maybe bullets, too.

Separation would be an intolerable situation for Canada and a reckless option for Quebec. Benefit would accrue only to certain parochial, myopic elites bent on self-aggrandizement. The "national question" is the principal means of organizing political thought in Quebec, guaranteeing eternal division between French and English citizens in that province as in the country as a whole. There is at present very little middle ground between extremes, and much of the francophone mass public seems momentarily more drawn to the rhetoric of ethnic and provincial primacy.

THE ENIGMA AND THE EXTRAS

Robert Bourassa: Dances with Polls

"Give me more love or more disdain;
The torrid or the frozen zone
Bring equal ease unto my pain,
The temperate affords me none;
Either extreme, of love or hate,
Is sweeter than a calm estate."

— from Mediocrity in Love Rejected
by Thomas Carew

Shakespeare's Macbeth declares no man "can be wise, amaz'd, temperate, and furious, loyal and neutral, in a moment." The Scottish King had never met Robert Bourassa. The ambivalence and ambiguity of the Quebec premier beggars parallel. Perhaps the worst poll-chaser since Gallup was a boy, Bourassa was ousted as premier by the separatist PQ in 1976, only to return from the wilderness to clear electoral victories. His metamorphosis from federalist to "protosovereignist" is not so grand as that of the butterfly, because Bourassa's convictions never made it out of their larval state. He is the *tabula rasa* of Canadian politics — the consummate politician whose canvas is as quickly erased as painted.

Of course, it would not be correct to claim that the Quebec premier does not stand for anything. His political career has been characterized by a single-minded advocacy of financial security for his province through hydro-electric power from the north. Bourassa's *maîtres chez nous* for the '90s is founded on relative economic independence, the core of which would still be the natural resources that have historically made Quebeckers hewers of wood and drawers of wages. But to realize the dream of energy billions and cheap power for local industries, two "tramplings" must take place. First, the fragile northern environment must be scarred and twisted with roads, settlements, dams, airports and spillways, despite growing public opposition to development "at any cost." Second, the lands, traditions and aspirations of aboriginal communities in the James Bay area must be shattered, perhaps forever. It is difficult to imagine what forces could prevent the Quebec government from continuing with the Great Whale phase of the James Bay project, and eventually beyond.

Bourassa is not enthralled by a policy of bilingualism. On the matter of giving fair treatment to the minority language spoken by three quarters of a million Quebeckers, the premier's record reads like a police blotter. The ham-handed and often silly sign law (Bill 178) has spawned cadres of linguistic brownshirts who march from block to block reporting to the authorities those evildoers who have not excised apostrophes or changed "hot dog" to "*chien chaud*." This law is driven less by cause than by pretext, as a means of momentarily mollifying xenophobic zealots. What has worked in Quebec as a sop to separatists has functioned in English Canada as a red flag in the faces of francophobes and decent folk alike. Bourassa's use of the constitutional override or "notwithstanding clause" to defend the sign law against vexatious liberty underscores how precarious are basic civil rights in all of Canada.

Much like his sometime adversaries the separatists, Bourassa perverts the notion of "*deux nations*." The biggest, most enduring and most damaging falsehood in the history of Canada is the fiction that the French Canadian nation corresponds to, and is contained only within the borders of, the province of Quebec. This gross misrepresentation of Canada's linguistic reality — a claim easily refuted with census data — is the cornerstone of the secessionist cause and a sacred cow among Quebec press and politicians. The official bilingualism introduced and entrenched in the Constitution by Trudeau expressed the understanding of an outstanding leader that all Canadians share in our joint heritage, and all Canadians, whether English- or French-speaking, are at home anywhere in this country. Until today, Robert Bourassa has been a much lesser man than the leaders of French Canada from Georges-Etienne Cartier to Wilfrid Laurier to Pierre Trudeau. It almost seems as if his political loyalty may be purchased with polling percentage points.

The variations and vicissitudes of Robert Bourassa are not merely infuriating, they could be destructive of Canadian unity. Some call him federalist, while others claim they know better. He dances with polls like Astaire with Rogers and sits mildly on the fence while the wind whispers, "maybe." A cartoonist once captured the true colours and true principles of Robert Bourassa in four simple words: "Make Me An Offer."

Robert Bourassa was the best hope Canada had in Quebec. His performance at the 1992 constitutional talks was low-key, moderate and just pro-Quebec enough that only the most extreme fringe of his Liberal party floated away. Leaked transcripts about the constitutional proceedings indicated he could have pushed harder for Quebec. With all the pressure on him from nationalists in his province he could have walked out of negotiations, but instead he contributed to the massive constitutional stew known as the Charlottetown accord. Unfortunately, in his attempt to please the other premiers, Prime Minister Mulroney and the majority of Quebeckers, he supported a flawed deal for the country which may yet prove to be his, and Canada's, undoing.

THE OTHERS

"I hold that man is in the right who is most closely in league with the future."

— Henrik Ibsen

While there are many other political leaders in Canada at present, they are of less importance than those who have been discussed so far. The support of a Triple-E Senate by the likes of Manitoba's Gary Filmon and Alberta's Don Getty had more to do with fear of the Reform Party than with any understanding of legislatures in Ottawa or abroad. This Senate scheme, which for a while became the new minimum "acceptable" condition for several provinces, was a powerful means of hideously exaggerating already troublesome divisions in national voting behaviour and the political orientations of electors. Gary Filmon is a classic example of the new urban flexible politician that plagues North American life. Don Getty (who promised to resign as premier after committing his colleagues to a hodge-podge, partially-elected Senate which grotesquely distorted "rep by pop," and which, when the numbers were right, would paralyze the federal government) should be classed as constitutionally "armed and dangerous."

Recent provincial elections have brought to the scene a trio of New Democrat premiers. While they have already had distinctiveDon effects on public life in their respective provinces, Roy Romanow of Saskatchewan, member of the 1981 "kitchen cabinet," has vastly more relevant experience than his comrades. Contrast Romanow's constitutional involvement through the years with that of the politically corrrect Bob Rae or British Columbia's trainee premier Michael Harcourt, who was ready to push issues such as gender equality beyond the bounds of common sense. Like Audrey McLaughlin, these three are heirs to a laudable social democratic tradition placing a high value on the ability of the state to intervene in the economy. Despite this, their recent actions speak of a cheerful acceptance of the dilution of federal power to the point where only provinces have any real say in how the country is run. Because they were upset with the antics of the current conservative/monetarist regime in Ottawa, these Mercedes Marxists participated in the emasculation of the federal Parliament. Perhaps the last vestiges of national vision among New Democrats have indeed been excised and replaced with the doctrine of "socialism in one province" wherever the opportunity happens to arise.

More than winds and waves batter the provinces of the Atlantic coast. Daily plant closures and dismal reports on fish stocks contribute to chronic unemployment and (relative to the other provinces) perpetual impoverishment. While the spirit of Maritimers may be indomitable, the economic and demographic significance of the eastern provinces has been in steady decline for a century. The commitment to Confederation is still strong, but sometimes suffers from creeping parochialism. Nova Scotia's Don Cameron appeared for a time to be unwilling to sacrifice the True North for the sake of Senate reform, but waffled and flipflopped during the crucial meetings leading up to the Charlottetown accord. Joe Ghiz of PEI, former constitutional lawyer and one of the few survivors of Meech Lake, still holds substantial influence in those matters that require provincial unanimity.

Meech assassin Clyde Wells has been clobbered by budget problems and the collapse of the northern cod fishery. He was too preoccupied with his ravaged Rock this time around to lash out against those who would reduce Parliament to an expensive debating society. Newfoundland does not need any more powers or jurisdictions, when it cannot afford those it has today. Though he may have despaired at the dice-rolling, this time he did not stand alone against the sequel to Meech.

Frank McKenna is the popular, practical, peacemaking premier of Canada's only officially bilingual province. The premier of New Brunswick understands the Constitution, and seems to know the players and the stakes. His clever companion resolution nearly saved Meech Lake, and he was active behind the scenes in reaching the flawed Charlottetown accord.

THE FIRST DUTY

Most people's eyes glazed over when, every single evening, they were brought the details of the latest bickering and whining in the constitution carnival. Virtually nothing of any merit was said as party leaders, cabinet ministers, provincial leaders and the talking heads of interest groups competed for attention. Tragic and comic was this circus of supreme law, where everyone stood up to be counted and nobody stood up for Canada.

All this was reminiscent of the play *The Doctors' Dilemma* by George Bernard Shaw. In this story, each of a number of physicians has a favourite remedy which he employs in every case, regardless of the patient's symptoms. In much the same way, Canada has politicians who see the answer to everything in a referendum or a Triple-E Senate, asymmetrical federalism or separation. The prescriptions scribbled out by many of our leaders are worse than the disease.

What makes Preston Manning, Lucien Bouchard and Jacques Parizeau dangerous to Canada is their approach to the difficult work of political compromise. None of them is interested in having to put more than the minimum effort into the task of cultural and constitutional accommodation. They all seek the destruction of the noble enterprise that is Canada.

All ten of our premiers have also failed to put Canada first and so have contributed to the coming crisis by legitimizing provincial, regional and ethnic parochialism. All ten are to be held accountable for the Charlottetown accord. They should have been reminded that the true leader is one who invites citizens to rise above provincial pride and perceived loss — to get on with the business of building this country.

Let us daily remind political leaders of their responsibility to keep Canada united under a strong federal government. Let us be firm in matters of principle, but malleable when it comes to rules and limits of authority. Let us not forget who are our friends and who are our enemies. It is from our friends that we demand the highest standards and the most stellar performance. It is difficult to be hard of nose without being hard of heart, but in this Canada must succeed. As freedom and fairness are our birthright, so vigilance and tolerance are our duty.

7 The Leadership Canada Deserves

"The conditions have always been difficult. We must pass through the barriers of languages and race, of geography and religion, of custom and tradition and we must build on a common foundation, without jealousy or hatred, with tolerance and sympathy."

— **Vincent Massey, Speaking of Canada**
(Toronto: Macmillan, 1959)

The challenge posed by former Governor-General Vincent Massey more than three decades ago is urgent today. The past generation of Canadians heeded his advice and passed through the barriers of race, geography, religion, custom and tradition and helped build a country of which we can justifiably be proud. This generation is in danger of losing that inheritance. What could make the difference between another prosperous and stable era and slipping backward into disunity and economic chaos is political leadership.

A federal election is quickly approaching and this one promises to be a watershed in Canadian history. Canadians will have an opportunity to pass judgment on the present government and choose new leaders worthy of our trust. We must take that mandate seriously, forcing would-be leaders to clarify their vision for Canada and explain how they propose to fulfill it. We should understand as well the inherent dangers of returning a weak, stalemate government based on a splintered Parliament. It may feel good to register dissatisfaction with the current government by voting for a regionally-based protest party, but at this point in history it could have dangerous consequences. If present opinion polling provides an accurate prediction, Canada's traditional two-and-a-half-party system will give way to five regional, narrowly-based parties with little in common. In such a case it is easy to forsee the possibility of Canada becoming almost ungovernable.

Despite a contemporary myth, Canada's overlapping problems are not caused by the diverse composition of Canadian society. They are not even caused by the problems of reforming the Constitution; these are only symptoms of the deeper problem. The real problems are the fading "idea of Canada" as a tolerant and just society and the new way we are learning to conceive of our differences. Assailed by distasteful events such as economic uncertainty, separatist agitation, demonstrations of bigotry, and harsh federal policies on trade and taxes, Canadians have developed an anger toward government which is understandable but also unprecedented. They have lost faith in the value of their politicians and political institutions. The shared vision of a strong, united country is being destroyed by the philosophy of difference, flawed institutions and weak leadership.

In an effort to escape from disillusionment with the federal democratic process, Canadians have shifted their loyalty from the larger state and its institutions to narrower frameworks for understanding political reality. In a search for belonging or community, the focus of loyalty has fragmented and moved to the separate bits and pieces of society. In other countries around the world this shift of loyalty has given rise to violent nationalism. In Canada the shift, so far, has been less dramatic. Canadians have come to see themselves first and foremost in terms of ethnicity, provincialism, regionalism and special interests. The conception of the country as a complete tapestry which weaves together various strands of ethnicity and regionalism, and is strengthened by its unity, has already been diminished.

These are the symptoms of decay. If we ignore them, decentralize the federal government and fragment the party system, it will be like pouring bleach all over our beautiful Canadian tapestry — the colours will fade, the threads will weaken, and eventually it will rip apart as it is pulled in all directions. Not even strong leadership then will be sufficient to ensure Canada's survival in the modern world.

IDEAS, INSTITUTIONS AND DISCORD

The ideology of difference has made Canada more difficult to govern. But it is not the only factor militating against pride in the democratic process and the ability to confront difficulties with optimism and unity. Canadians are also discovering that many of their institutions are flawed. And not all of the flaws can be resolved by constitutional amendments. The Prime Minister and Cabinet are too authoritarian. Parliament is too weak and is losing ground to the executive. The Constitution does not meet the needs of today's changing society. The media feeds public cynicism by conveying the message that all authority and leadership is bad. Politicians and political leaders make the largest headlines when they are in conflict of interst, or worse yet, downright corrupt.

During this decade of rapid decay in public pride and weakening institutions, Canadian leadership has been barely adequate to keep the ship of state afloat. Our present Prime Minister has deviated from the progressive policies of earlier leaders, both Liberal and Conservative. Unlike his predecessors Mr. Mulroney does not accept the triad of federal authority — that there must be a strong central government, that on occasion the federal government may have to interfere in a comprehensive manner in the economy, and that it is the responsibility of the federal government to ensure a universal social security system to reach those who are weak, handicapped, old, sick, unemployed, or otherwise disadvantaged.

Since we are watching these cornerstones of our country being gradually but deliberately chipped away, it is no wonder individual Canadians are disconsolate and searching for lower level and narrower institutions to protect their interests.

Despite these difficulties the federal government and all provincial premiers advocate reforming the Constitution holus-bolus. The Conservative government prefers an agreement which satisfies all of the premiers, especially Quebec, and assure a Conservative victory in the next general election. But Canadians should be aware that this may be no more than short-sighted politics. Such an agreement might help the Conservatives win the next general election, but if it weakens the central government and makes governing more difficult in the future, such an agreement would be bad for Canada. The federal government appears unconcerned about whether or not proposed new institutional arrangements will work effectively to make Canada a more prosperous, just and free country. Yet these should be the foremost criteria by which all constitutional proposals are measured, not by whether they are acceptable to politicians who have personal axes to grind or selfish gains to make.

The Prime Minister is willing to undertake a new and dangerous experiment with the Canadian Constitution. He forgets that a constitution is not only about laws and institutions but is about individuals, families and groups whose daily lives are affected by the activities of government. A constitution should not be tampered with without precise knowledge of where the changes will lead.

The Charlottetown constitutional proposals would decentralize the country even more than it already is — move it from one of the most decentralized federal systems in the world to by far the most decentralized. If they weaken Ottawa, strengthen the provinces and enhance the role of ethnic groups and special interests, our leaders will leave the country with a gridlock of institutions and a do-nothing government. It will not matter much which party wins the next general election because the new government will be in a straight-jacket. When the latest constitutional proposals are combined with a five-party, divided Parliament the central government, which is the only institution to make decisions for all of Canada, will be weaker still. The changes would make it more difficult for the federal government to stand up to a separatist government in the future.

THE DECAYING PARTY SYSTEM

Canada's two-and-a-half-party system is eroding quickly, as the Bloc Québécois and the Reform Party sap the support of the older, established parties. The two new parties are blessed with militants, money and a simple message. With the decay of the two major parties — Liberals and Conservatives — as organizations which can aggregate the various ethnic groups and interests of the country, and with the New Democratic Party unable to create a new bridge between French- and English-speaking populations or to gain any significant support in Atlantic Canada, we are headed to a multi-party system in which the federal government will be based on only a minority of members of Parliament or a weak coalition.

The old two-and-a-half-party system with the Conservatives and Liberals followed by the NDP continues to have moderate appeal. But as the polling data in Figure 7:1 show, the new Bloc Québécois and Reform parties have gained considerably in the past two years. And what is even more important than their overall strength is that these two parties are exceptionally powerful in two provinces — Quebec and Alberta. While it is true that polls taken before an election are not reliable guides to the actual votes which will be cast, the fact that the economic recession and the national unity crisis continue means that heavy voting for each of the five parties can be predicted with confidence. To guess the details of the electoral outcome, however, remains a speculative and sensitive exercise.

The Bloc Québécois, led by Lucien Bouchard, campaigns openly for Quebec's complete independence. If it does not disband because of an Ottawa-Quebec rapprochement on the Constitution, it could do extremely well in Quebec during a general election. Certainly in a two-party fight for the Quebec nationalist vote, the Progressive Conservatives would find their 1984 and 1988 strength severely diminished. In the West, especially in Alberta and British Columbia, and scattered in a few other English-speaking provinces, the Reform party of Canada led by Preston Manning has sapped the strength of the Conservative Party. Reform also has a natural ally in the anti-bilingual Confederation of Regions (CORE) party in other areas, especially in the Maritimes.

Figure 7:1 Party Reference

Trends in Support for Federal Parties

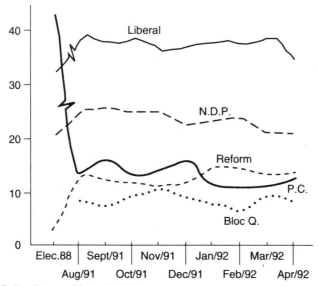

SOURCE: Gallup Report, 23 April 1992
The question asked was: "If a federal election were held today, which party's candidate do you think you would favour?"

219

The framentation of the vote among five parties will not take place in all regions of the country. As in the past, in some areas two- or three-party splits will dominate. But at least two regions will have four-party divisions. The single member plurality (first-past-the-post) electoral system will be of great significance in the outcome when this occurs. In regions with four-party contests, an even split would mean that a party with only 26% of the vote could obtain all the seats, or none of them, depending on the precise configuration of the vote.

Imagine what Canada could look like after the next election if current trends continue: British Columbia and Saskatchewan would be Reform and NDP; Alberta would vote mostly Reform and a little Conservative; Quebec would have a mixture of Bloc Québécois, Conservatives and Liberals; the Maritimes would still vote mainly Liberal; and Manitoba and Ontario would probably be a Liberal, Conservative and NDP mix.

Following their penchant for personalities, divisive issues and episodic politics, journalists have distracted public attention from this over-all picture to the smaller one — the details of Reform Party policy, the antics of the Bloc Québécois, squabbles and leaks about the referendum and so on. It is time to adjust that focus and consider the *overall pattern* of what could happen to Canada if five parties share the vote in the next election.

National parties, which unite Canadians from all provinces in a common direction, may become extinct after the next election. Taking their place will be several small, fragmented regional parties which, to varying degrees, promote and appeal to regional, populist interests. In short, Canada may be headed toward a hodge-podge of parties not unlike that found in Italy, where short-lived coalition governments have resulted. Italy now has its 50th new government since World War II — over three times as many as Canada has had during the same period. Since 1946, Italy's governments have lasted only about 10 months on average, and the passing of each has been marked by parades of scandals, political plots and high-decibel rhetoric.

If the adoption of a multi-party system with its coalition governments causes similar turnover in Canada, politics will be totally transformed. For example, since the last election in 1988 we would already have had about five new governments — with different leaders, policies and regional support each time. With such a government the country would be in even worse shape than it is today. In short, government would become even more expensive, less efficient, more partisan and less responsive than it is now.

Italian coalition governments do not seem to present a problem in terms of economic prosperity for that country; the peninsular state is doing reasonably well economically. However, it is doubtful if Canada could do as well given the same conditions. Italy has a unitary form of government, and although there are impressive regional differences, the regions do not have strong provincial governments which can challenge the central authority. As well, one language dominates political life, and varieties of ethnicity and regionalism do not distract Italians from knowing who they are as a people.

Of course, coalition governments are not always unstable. Some smaller European democracies such as Austria, the Netherlands and Switzerland manage just fine. However, these are "consociational" democracies — countries which possess a strong coalition spirit across the leadership of the parties. With little fanfare and no rancour, the leaders of the different parties join in coalitions in order to run the country. There is no evidence that such spiritual cohesion exists in Canadian government and politics. Small parties simply have not played a crucial role at the federal level. Canadians have retained a single member, plurality electoral system because of a preference for the stability of two broad, national parties rather than the politics of coalition.

In the past in Canada, the Liberal and Conservative parties have prevented the proliferation of smaller parties by attacking and infiltrating them. A good example was the farmer's Progressive Party which appeared briefly on the national scene in the 1920s. When the Progressives drew up their party platform in 1918, the Liberals stole a large percentage of it. And Mackenzie King missed no occasion to woo Progressives until they splintered into three groups, were absorbed into larger parties and finally eliminated as an independent political force.

Canadian federal governments, almost without exception, have been formed from relatively homogeneous groups within the same political party. It is generally believed among experts that such homogeneity creates efficiency, consistent leadership, internal cohesiveness and government durability. Canadian politicians have viewed coalition governments with suspicion. Since Confederation, Canada has had only one explicit coalition — the Union Government led by Sir Robert Borden — which was formed during the First World War to enforce the terms of the Conscription Act of 1917. This Borden coalition government worked quite smoothly while the war lasted, but as soon as the urgency to cooperate disappeared, the spirit of conciliation and compromise died and the coalition disintegrated.

Pizza politics is probably coming to Canada. Before we are saddled with five or more regionally-based parties, Canadians should reflect on the overall pattern of politics they are encouraging and decide if that is what they really favour. The relationship between national party politics and the handling of constitutional issues is vital to the future of the country.

CONSTITUTIONAL ISSUES

Constitutional change, by its very nature, should be a difficult, slow process that cannot be manipulated at the whim of a single government — in Ottawa, Quebec or any other province. Constitutions should be difficult to amend. Changes should emerge from a genuine consensus among governments and the people.

The political challenge is to write a constitution that obtains the right balance. The proposals must do two things. They must keep Quebec in Canada and also make it possible to govern effectively. If too little is done Quebec may separate. If too much is given away by the federal government it may not be possible to govern the country. The decentralization demands of the regions — particularly as articulated by those who believe Canada would be better off with "Deconfederation" — are better left to be debated in the ivory towers of some universities. There is very little fundamentally wrong with the Constitution as it is, and a grand social experiment is something the country does not need. Five basic principles should guide judgments about constitutional revision:

First, amendments should enhance the probability of the country staying together, not reinforce cleavages that already exist or create new ones. They should express common ideals and values, not the philosophy of difference.

Second, amendments should reinforce the strength of the federal government: the central institutions should be constructed so that they will work effectively when there is a majority *or* a minority government, and they should reinforce the federal government's ability to confront a secessionist provincial administration.

Third, amendments should explicitly defend the rights of all individuals within Canadian society. Collective rights are also part of the Canadian heritage and are imbedded in the present Constitution. They should be maintained in a balanced form; there should be no hierarchy of rights in which some groups profit more than others.

Fourth, amendments ought to protect the weak and disadvantaged in Canadian society. Countries are, and should be, judged by how well they care for the least fortunate individuals and groups among them.

Finally, amendments should allow the federal government to act effectively in the economy to protect our economic prosperity, enforce a free trade within the country, and make Canada an effective player in the new global economy.

As we demonstrated in Chapter 5, the Charlottetown accord does not uphold these five principles.

The fifth principle is particularly important today because of Canada's continuing recession, a fiscal crisis, declining economic competitiveness and the possible long-term deleterious affect of the Free Trade Agreement with the United States (FTA) and the new, as yet unratified, North American Free Trade Agreement (NAFTA). The FTA constituted a major step toward dismantling the system of government Canada has built up over the years. It represented a "declaration of dependence" on our southern neighbour which, coupled with a more decentralized constitution, will reduce the power of the federal government and undermine the very foundations of government action.

With the Free Trade Agreement in place, Canadians need a strong federal government that will speak with one voice for the economic interests of all Canadians, not one which is crippled or weakened by provincial perogatives. The Charlottetown accord does not meet adequately the criteria of the above five principles for constitutional revision. It is divisive both in content and in the rigid manner in which it was presented. The accord does not explicitly defend a strong federal government and builds rigidity and uncertainty into the Constitution. The proposals reduce the federal government's capacity to act decisively in economic and social policy and may lead to the long-term erosion of federal authority.

In principle, the language and culture provisions of the Charlottetown accord are acceptable. The details were best covered in the unanimous, all-party Charest parliamentary committee report which was shelved over two years ago. It clarified Meech Lake and made the proposals meaningful and practical. Given the political situation today, the Charlottetown proposals which relate to protection of the French language and culture in Quebec, and to protection of minority language groups throughout the country, should be tolerated. By contrast, we should not accept a massive transfer of powers to Quebec or any other province or disrupt the political system by a wholesale change in political institutions. We should retain those powers and institutions in Ottawa which have given us effective economic and social policy in the past. In the future we shall need such federal authority in order to create a child-care policy, protect the environment, and improve post-secondary education funding to mention only a few contemporary issues.

Referendums: The New Panacea?

During the past couple of years the idea of a referendum has paraded as a popular panacea for constitutional problems. Our governments have brandished referendums as veiled threats to each other. Quebec was scheduled to hold one by October 26, 1992; British Columbia and Alberta decided to hold referendums before accepting any constitutional amendments; Saskatchewan and Newfoundland suggested they might call their own referendums; and in the spring of 1992 the federal Parliament finally passed a law making a national referendum possible.

Referendums have a long history but have been invoked only sporadically in Canada. "Plebiscite" — the older term — came from the vote of the plebs in Rome in the 4th century BC. It was used to refer to popular consultations in France from 1793 onward. "Referendum" appeared in the 1880s in England, earlier in Switzerland.

In Canada, the two terms are loosely used, often to mean the same thing. It is generally considered that there are two kinds of referendums. Some are legally binding in that they force the government to enact legislation according to the majority decision whether or not the government agrees with the results. Others, really plebicites, are merely consultative. These are, in essence, glorified opinion polls. They have no legal, binding nature, so governments feel free to ignore them if they do not like the way they turn out.

Referendums have serious deficiencies that make them rarities at the national level in liberal democracies — and for justifiable reasons. Only about 500 are known to have been held in the whole history of the world, and over half of them were in one country — Switzerland. The United States has never held any at all at the national level.

Theory and practice are far apart. Whenever a referendum is employed, it should bear a clear, cautionary label, like cigarettes, saying that it could be dangerous to the health of the country. Referendums are just a government's procedural tool and are as open to abuse as any other procedure. There are many myths about them.

The first supposed benefit of both types of referendums is that they allow for wide participation — for unadulterated, direct democracy. They allow the public to bypass their political representatives who may or may not accurately represent their opinions. When a population has the opportunity to vote in a referendum it gives an air of legitimacy to the decision. For that reason it is sometimes argued that such devices are a good mechanism for ratifying fundamental decisons.

Authoritarian leaders tend to be aware of this legitimation process and often use referendums to manipulate demonstrations of support. They can be blatantly propagandist as well as genuinely democratic. Authoritarian regimes often produce referendums with massive majorities of 99%. But more often than not such impressive results are achieved by false information and intimidation.

Adolph Hitler loved referendums. They suited his intentions perfectly. He stirred populist emotions on nationalism and racism and used referendums to legitimize one of the most genuinely wicked regimes in history. He never achieved less than a 92% affirmation in his referendums. What a commentary on direct democracy! The point is that public opinion is easily swayed and cannot necessarily be relied on to make a wise decision at any particular point in time.

There is a second related myth about referendums: that they allow the people to decide policy and that such participation is good. However, not all referendums do allow citizens to decide. Sometimes they are legally binding, but often — and so far *always* at the national level in Canada — they are just glorified opinion polls. Governments feel free to ignore the results if they so choose.

Moreover, direct participation is not necessarily a positive thing. Decisions made by citizens are not always fair or just merely because a majority support them. This is particularly true if voter turnout in the referendum is small, so that the result is not truly representative. There have been many occasions in democracies and non-democracies when public opinion was easily manipulated and distorted by unscrupulous leaders. This is particularly easy to do when questions of ethnicity or minority groups are involved.

Also, many of the problems facing modern governments are complex and demanding and require more time and energy than most citizens are willing to spend on them. Relatively uninformed citizens may not want, or be able, to make a wise choice on a complex issue. A referendum such as a government proposal on a constitutional package is incredibly complex, with many propositions about the mangement of the country hidden inside it. All political arguments consist of compounds of preferences and values and a simple yes/no is rarely appropriate. And after all, that is why we go to all the expense of electing paid representatives to look after the national interest in the first place.

Still a third myth is that referendums solve bitter and divisive national disputes democratically and therefore definitively and without rancour. Nothing could be further from the truth. For one thing, referendums by their very nature cannot weigh the intensity of the beliefs behind a vote. Votes in favour of an issue may express unenthusiastic marginal preferences while negative votes may represent passionate opposition. In such a case if the pro-votes win, the losers are likely to pursue the matter afterwards as a gross injustice. Because of the yes/no, winner-take-all nature of referendums there is no way to compromise or break up an issue into more palatable portions which can satisfy more people. If the government acts on a referendum it endorses total victory for one side, total defeat for the other. Representative democracy, in which politicians are placed between the public and law-makers, offers more possibilities of compromise politics between the extremes of an issue.

Referendums are often used to overrule the interests of minorities. The yes/no responses and inability to measure intensity of beliefs behind the vote work against minorities. For example, some states in the United States have held referendums which overturned laws prohibiting discrimination against blacks and women. When compromises are not reached, and the will of a majority is forced on an aggrieved minority, an issue does not go away. We saw that after the 1980 Quebec referendum. A 60% majority of Quebeckers voted to stay in Canada, but barely a decade later the issue is back. Nothing was solved by the referendum.

In Canada, we have conducted two referendums at the federal level, neither of which can be construed as successful. Both were consultative, and both pitted French against English. The first was in 1898, when the federal government was contemplating prohibition of alcohol. Fifty-one percent voted in favour, but Prime Minister Laurier said that too few people cast their votes and ignored the result. The turnout had been low, and besides, Quebec was strongly against the prohibition and it would have been bad electoral politics to proceed.

The second national referendum was during the Conscription Crisis of 1942. Sixty-five percent of the vote favoured conscription and the government went ahead with it. But again, Quebec was strongly against the proposal and the bitterness which ensued coloured English-French relations for decades.

In Canada referendums are more commonly used at lower government levels; practically all provinces and many municipalities have held referendums on issues such as alcohol and fluoridation. And, of course, it is the method by which Newfoundland chose to join the country in 1949 — although it took two tries to accomplish the act.

In a federal country like Canada referendums are complicated further by the existence of federal and provincial jurisdictions. Provincial governments, for example, would be incensed if the federal government were to hold a referendum which infringed on their jurisdictions — say on education or health care. However, Quebec obviously feels no compunction to restrict its own referendums to provincial fields of jurisdiction. A referendum on sovereignty affects the integrity of the entire country.

Experiences of countries such as Australia which use legally binding referendums as the means by which to make constitutional amendments should be studied carefuly. When the Australian public has been given the opportunity to vote on constitutional issues it has almost always opted for the status quo. Thirty out of 38 constitutional referendums have been turned down since 1906. It would not be surprising if voters in a Canadian referendum also concluded that the status quo is better than the government-sponsored constitutional proposals.

Referendums are intended to bestow an air of legitimacy on the government's choice of action. Governments hold them when they believe the public will give them a resounding vote of approval to proceed according to plan. The public is fickle and governments take advantage of fluctuations in opinion to choose the time when they expect to win.

Referendums are not entirely without redeeming features, but they do have severe, and sometimes dangerous, limitations. We should be aware of what is myth and what is reality.

MASKING THE TRUTH

Despite the overwhelming evidence that referendums divide populations into hostile camps, the Canadian government called a national referendum on the Charlottetown proposals for October 26, 1992. Our leaders say this process will avert a major constitutional crisis. Their argument is shortsighted and politically motivated. The process and content of the deal will create the conditions for a much more serious crisis and make the break-up of Canada more likely.

The decision to hold a national referendum was naive because it did not consider the pressures from the three major fault lines and the public's lack of confidence in today's leaders and political institutions. Given the problems inherent in referendums, an election should have been called instead.

The referendum is an unnecessary and expensive public relations trick on Canadians which is in keeping with the Mulroney strategy to kill us with kindness. Its results are not legally binding on anyone. Even if the referendum obtains a majority of votes in every province and the country as a whole, the 11 legislatures will still have to approve the deal.

Canadians are being asked to approve a set of principles rather than a finalized legal text. The agreement is a list of deals — many of which are vague and contradictory. Some clauses may not even be possible to put into legal language. We are being asked to vote for a "pig in a poke." When the government was told there was an omission in the Canada Clause concerning handicapped people, Joe Clark responded, "If the referendum is approved we can add it later." Can they add anything else they want once the referendum is approved?

This referendum will be divisive and never should have been called. A better option would have been a vote on a single constitutional issue rather than one on such an unwieldy package. And if the federal government could not come up with a restricted amendment it ought to have called a general election. The current federal government has no electoral mandate to dismantle the established constitutional framework.

There are to be two steps in the constitutional proceedings. First, there is the referendum on the Charlottetown accord which is supported by the federal government, the ten provincial premiers, and the leaders of the territorial and aboriginal groups. Second, if the referendum is approved, identical constitutional resolutions will have to be passed in all ten legislatures and the Parliament of Canada.

There are no rules about what the consequences of the referendum will be. Since the vote is only advisory and not legally binding, governments may treat it in any way they desire. If one province, in particular Quebec, votes "no," does that mean what the whole referendum has been defeated? Probably yes. But we simply do not know.

Other federal countries have more precise rules for constitutional change. The standard formula is that a referendum result is not accepted unless approved by a double-majority formula which requires a vote of 50% of the total population *and* a majority of the provinces containing half of the population.

In Canada, no one knows for certain what the referendum results will mean unless there is a majority for it in every province and in the country as a whole. In Quebec, Alberta and British Columbia there is provincial legislation which will make it extremely difficult for the premiers to go against what the people decide. Elsewhere it is less clear as the politicians have avoided being pinned down by regulations or laws.

If, as may happen, Quebec votes "no" but the rest of the country votes "yes," we will be in a crisis. This is why we should never have had a referendum. We should not misjudge Quebec. A high percentage of the intellectual elite wants some form of sovereignty or independence. Polls show that the mass population is divided, but that a growing number accept some form of sovereignty. The chance that Quebec will vote against the Mulroney constitutional package is extremely high. If this occurs Canada will face the crisis that we all wanted to avoid. There may have to be *another* purely Quebec referendum as in 1980 in order to force Quebeckers to choose between independence and loyalty to Canada.

Canadians are being asked to give a simple yes or no answer to the most massive re-drafting of the Constitution that this country has ever conducted.

We must not allow ourselves to be coralled mindlessly into the yes camp "just to get it all over with" or because we are told it is the patriotic thing to do. We should judge the tentative deal and vote yes or no on its merits. It will be a very difficult task, as the government's propaganda campaign is immense. This time Brian Mulroney has loaded the dice. Unlike the procedure for general elections, the referendum law allows the government to fund its own cause with taxpayers' money.

Educators must judge students by what they produce on their essays and exams, not by whether or not they like the student or the student's father might cause a fuss if an "A" grade is not awarded. We should examine the Charlottetown proposals in the same way. If the deal stands up to scrutiny we should vote yes. If it does not, we should vote "no." Other pressures should be ignored.

Our leaders say that if we vote "yes" the debilitating constitutional debate will end and we can finally concentrate on solving other urgent problems like the economy. They say that if we vote no we will have voted for constitutional chaos and the break-up of Canada.

It is a lie. They are masking the trust.

As we have clearly shown in Chapter 5, the deal our leaders are proposing will irrevocably change the face of Canada, and they are not even sure how. Brian Mulroney once boasted that the resolution of the country's constitutional "crisis" would be his ticket to re-election. The country does not need this agreement nearly as badly as Mr. Mulroney does.

What a "yes" vote really means is a vote for a massive ambiguous document that received agreement by giving away federal powers that have historically been used to keep a strong federal government that can provide equal services to all Canadians. It is a vote to enshrine in our Constitution an incomprehensible patchwork of competing, irreconcilable interests. It is a vote to enshrine the philosophy of difference, and a hierarchy of rights for different groups as a new guiding principle and fundamental value. A "yes" vote is a vote to weaken Canada.

A "no" vote can mean many things. For thoughtful Canadians it is the only avenue that has been given to say — "hold on, we are moving too fast into uncharted waters." There are some good ideas in the Charlottetown accord, but there is much that we do not understand and that could threaten all that we have built up and enjoy in this great country. There are some provisions that we already know are inherently wrong for Canada. If they are entrenched in the Constitution it will be impossible to change them and return to where we are now. The Charlottetown accord includes a veto for every province. In the future, a separatist government or one hostile province could bind us to the Charlottetown mistake. If our leaders can't fix problem areas now without ruining the compromise, it will surely be impossible later.

"No" puts a stop to Mr. Mulroney's ticket to re-election. it means "try again, even though it is painful. Canada is worth it." It means that even though the political elites of this country have banded together in favour of this accord, ordinary Canadians can read the preliminary document, think for themselves and exercise their democratic right to say "this is not good enough."

Canadians have been placed in the incongruous position of having to vote "no" in order to stand up for their country.

What Happens If We Vote Yes

The final text will have to be produced and agreed on by the 11 legislatures of Canada. This will provide a further opportunity for the "no" side to struggle to be heard and stop this badly flawed deal. A new round of Constitutional wrangling will begin almost immediately as politicians clash over what the ambiguous words, contradictory ideas and clauses really mean.

Will Canada still work if Canada votes "yes" and the Charlottetown accord is entrenched in the Canadian Constitution?

The simple answer is that it will, but only until significant problems arise. And that could be in the very near future. As soon as there is a minority government in Ottawa, five competing political parties in Parliament, and/or a separatist government in Quebec, the country will founder. Separation will be much more likely. We will almost have guaranteed the break-up of the country.

Separatism in Quebec will not go away. We cannot appease nationalists with anything but complete independence for Quebec. There are about a million and a quarter of them. They are only a minority in that province, but a majority of the political elite. We cannot allow them to continually hold the country to ransom with their demands.

If we approve the Charlottetown accord, we will decentralize the country further than it already is, and that will be a great mistake. A country which encompasses so many diverse interests needs a strong, unifying government. The late constitutional guru and great Canadian, Senator Eugene Forsey, decried such efforts to turn the central government into little more than a referee and chief cashier. It would be, he said, like "10 jackasses eating the leaves off a single maple tree." We would add that when the leaves are all gone there will be no food and no shade left for any of them.

If the vote is "yes," Mulroney will claim victory. Problems in the accord will not yet be apparent, and Mulroney will use it as the launching pad for the coming general election.

What Happens If We Vote No

Canada will *not* fall apart if the "no" forces win. There will be an election in 1993, and a new team with new ideas will tackle the problem of Constitutional reform.

If there is a "no" vote in any province in Canada there will be only one democratic solution. There will have to be a general election to determine which leaders can take the country forward. There is no doubt that throughout the period since Meech Lake the Prime Minister has wanted a *perceive* constitutional success — one which would give him his window to quit or run again. (In 1983 he claimed he only wanted two mandates.) In the final analysis his strategic, labour-lawyer approach forced him to accept the Charlottetown accord with all its warts and dangers for Canada. Canada is already suffering for it.

DIVIDED WE FALL

It was "to begin with...a toy, an amusement; then it became a mistress, and then a master, and then a tyrant." Winston Churchill was reflecting on book-writing when he made this comment, but he could easily have been referring to Canadian politicians writing a constitution. It may have begun as only a minor task, but eventually it has overwhelmed those involved. What began as "renewed federalism" — a gesture of goodwill for Quebec — has become a master and tyrant.

Given what is now known about the contours of Canadian politics — the overlapping problems based on several fault lines, low confidence in institutions and politicians, weak leadership at the centre and the possibility of five-party representation in the House of Commons — it is clear that the country needs strong central government institutions in Ottawa that can withstand periods of extreme challenge.

Canada is a thinly populated federal country in a very large, competitive world. The globe is becoming more complex because of integration in trade, investments, technology, communications and even weapons systems. Our country faces greater and greater competition from states which are more highly centralized and disciplined than Canada. And yet, many of our leaders propose to decentralize the country even more than it already is.

Canadians rank among the healthiest, wealthiest and luckiest people on earth. But what we enjoy today is the result of yesterday's effort and success. We should not massively overhaul institutions and procedures that are not broken. And we should be suspicious of politicians who tell us we should. If we want to pass on our benefits to the next generation we must preserve what is good, and stop our perpetual introspection and bickering.

It is time to put behind us the ideology of difference and heal the country's political institutions. These tasks may well require a new set of politicians. When given the opportunity in the next general election we should ask potential leaders how they would tackle the issues which arise from Canada's fault lines. The best leaders will be those brave enough to discard the ideology of difference and renew our faith in government's capacity to solve problems of constitutional conflict, economic stability and social justice. They will be the friends of Canada.

Canada is like a ship — probably it will not sink, but those aboard will often get wet in stormy weather. If we are not terrified of capsizing we will be able to plot a better course and use the political currents to our advantage. There are always some who would profit if the ship founders. Nothing bothers rats more than when a ship fails to sink. They are the enemies of Canada.

Canadians can adjust the Constitution to accommodate the demands of a pluralistic society but we must do it in a slow, deliberate, incremental manner. We have most to lose if we accept the Charlottetown accord without understanding its implications, and inadvertently and irrevocably alter the nature of our country. This constitutional amendment would weaken the federal government, leave it unable to meet the demands of separatists in the future, and unable to act on behalf of all Canadians; it would undermine the *Charter of Rights and Freedoms;* and it would threaten our identity as a compassionate and tolerant unified, bilingual and bicultural nation.

By disagreeing with the accord we must not follow conservative bigots or left-leaning intellectuals who say we can survive without Quebec. If Quebec leaves it will not be the tolerant, world-class Canada we know. If the country elects a five-party parliament with a weak, stalemate government it sill not be able to keep Canada together. In either case, it will be an unworthy legacy for those we love. We will have failed.

It is time to put aside our differences and stand up for Canada. In the words of the poet W.B. Yeats we ask our political leaders on behalf of every Canadian, "tread softly, because you tread on my dreams."

SOURCES

p. 113   Erik H. Erikson on Hitler in Erikson, Erik H., *Childhood and Society*, 3rd ed. (New York: Norton, 1963).

Erich Fromm on Hitler in Fromm, Erich, *The Anatomy of Human Destructiveness* (London: Holt, 1977).

Robert Tucker on Stalin in Tucker, Robert, *Stalin in Power* (New York: Norton, 1990).

Harold Lasswell concepts from Lasswell, Harold, *Power and Personality* (New York: Norton, 1948) p. 3.

p. 122   "In politics one has to do..." quoted in Donaldson, Gordon, *Eighteen Men: The Prime Ministers of Canada* (Toronto: Doubleday, 1985) p. 157.

p. 127   "Canadian political discontent..." from Dobell, Peter and Berry, Byron, "Anger at the System: Political Discontent in Canada," *Parliamentary Government*, no. 39 (1992) p. 5.

p. 185   "Preston Manning is the flip side..." quote by Jean Chrétien, "Federal Forum," Liberal Party of Canada, Spring 1992.